An Untold Story

An Untold Story

Heroism, Mysticism, and the Quest for the True Self

Robert C. Pelfrey

CASCADE *Books* · Eugene, Oregon

AN UNTOLD STORY
Heroism, Mysticism, and the Quest for the True Self

Cascade Books
An Imprint of Wipf and Stock Publishers
199 W. 8th Ave., Suite 3
Eugene, OR 97401

www.wipfandstock.com

PAPERBACK ISBN: 978-1-6667-5133-8
HARDCOVER ISBN: 978-1-6667-5134-5
EBOOK ISBN: 978-1-6667-5135-2

Cataloguing-in-Publication data:

Names: Pelfrey, Robert C., author.

Title: An untold story : heroism, mysticism, and the quest for the true self / Robert C. Pelfrey.

Description: Eugene, OR : Cascade Books, 2023 | Includes bibliographical references.

Identifiers: ISBN 978-1-6667-5133-8 (paperback) | ISBN 978-1-6667-5134-5 (hardcover) | ISBN 978-1-6667-5135-2 (ebook)

Subjects: LCSH: Spiritual formation. | Spirituality—Christianity—History—Middle Ages, 600–1500. | Heroes—Religious aspects—Christianity. | Ruusbroec, Jan van, 1293–1381.

Classification: BV5095.J3 P45 2023 (print) | BV5095.J3 P45 (ebook)

JANUARY 24, 2023 11:33 AM

In loving memory of my father, Michael Pelfrey (1938–2022),
whose own heroic journey has now led him
across the High Sea and beyond the mountains
to explore the endless Empyrean

"But Larry," she smiled. "People have been asking those questions for thousands of years. If they could be answered, surely they'd have been answered by now."

" . . . It's not true that no one has found the answers. There are more answers than questions, and lots of people have found answers that were perfectly satisfactory for them. Old Ruusbroec for instance."

"Who was he?"

"Oh, just a guy I didn't know at college," Larry answered flippantly.

—W. Somerset Maugham, *The Razor's Edge*

CONTENTS

ACKNOWLEDGMENTS

T HE RESEARCH THAT GREW into this book was largely conducted at the University of Manchester; Nazarene Theological College and the Manchester Wesley Research Centre in Manchester, England; and the Ruusbroec Institute at the University of Antwerp, Belgium. I am grateful for the faculty and staff at these glorious centers of learning. I am also appreciative of the community of scholars in the Mystical Theology Network.

I've been blessed to develop and practice the theology of spiritual formation presented in this book as a pastor in the Northwest Texas and New Mexico Annual Conferences of the United Methodist Church. I am thankful for the many committed sojourners, both lay and clergy, who inspire and share in this work of making disciples.

This stretch of my journey has found me in the sterling company of a band of wise, loving, funny, godly men. I am deeply grateful for my fellow *Hemelbesems*—Gerard Booy, Daniel Harris, and Dan Miller. I couldn't ask for hardier travel companions.

Finally, home is wherever Jamie and Maddie Jane are—the warmth of hearth and hearts, the cheer of laughter and music, and the place where they have to take me in. They are models of heroism and the most dependable sources of the divine embrace in my sometimes-fraught adventure. It is the blessing of my life to journey with them.

Soli Deo Gloria

INTRODUCTION

There is no greater agony than bearing an untold story inside you.

—Maya Angelou, *I Know Why the Caged Bird Sings*

R ECENTLY I WAS READING a bit of my family's story. My maternal great-grandmother, upon whose lap I sat as a child, was a Choctaw born in the Choctaw Nation (Oklahoma) in 1885. Her grandfather, upon whose lap she sat as a child, came to Indian Territory after being forced with his wife and young son to leave their home in Mississippi and walk the Trail of Tears around 1832. His grandparents, and their grandparents, and so on, all lived and traveled and played and fought and worshiped and loved in the land for centuries before America was ever "discovered." I can only imagine the adventures they had and the many stories they could tell. And all of this comprises only a few shoots on one limb of my family tree.

Each of us is the result of thousands of ancestors and, so, thousands of stories. Most of those stories were not the stuff of cinematic blockbusters (though some certainly were!). But they were the stories of real flesh-and-soul people with faces and voices and hopes and struggles and the whispered or shouted call to a dynamic relationship with the living God. With such storied beginnings, surely we have the potential to experience each chapter, each season, and most days and moments of our lives as breathing in and out with that same God. Perhaps we even have the potential to live as a divine revelation among our own contemporaries. This would be to live as our true selves, and to tell our true stories.

Within us, through us, and around us, God is present, God is living and breathing, and God is acting. This is the initial situation for our adventure, the setting of our calling. We needn't be anywhere else or anyone else to receive this Call. God can call us only where we are and as we are. But we can be sure: God is calling.

I had a conversation with a colleague a few years ago in which we were discussing our respective research. At one point during my explanation of life with God as a heroic journey, my mild-mannered friend exclaimed in frustration, "Not all of us can be heroes!" I imagine that sentiment is shared by many, and I'm convinced it's the result of a misunderstanding of the concept of heroism. It's true that one of the pioneering scholars of heroism studies, Thomas Carlyle (1795–1881), built his heroic ideal on the notion that true heroism is found only in the history and deeds of "Great Men."[1] Tragically, such a view is highly exclusionary when it comes to potential heroes, and was even used by Carlyle and some of his adherents to support anti-abolitionist, anti-democratic, and anti-Semitic views.

But the truth is that most heroic stories, in the Bible, for example, are about people who were anything but what would be considered hero material. This continued to be true of many people across history who would go on to become known for their deep faith and profound godliness and heroic fruitfulness, but whose initial potential would strike no one as especially dazzling. And yet, surely most of us tend to find the most memorable expressions of heroism in the underdogs of history and storytelling. So, no, I'm not suggesting we are ready-made heroes just stalking one adventure after another. It's the Call, the One who calls, and our response to both that forms the raw stuff of our potential into a truly heroic life.

If we are suspicious about the suggestion of being a hero, we might also question the idea of being a mystic. And we will likely doubt the relationship between the two. After all, aren't heroes people of action, and mystics typically naval-gazers who are so heavenly minded that they're no earthly good? How could a mystic be a hero, and vice versa? We might also think of mysticism as mostly the domain of Eastern traditions like Zen Buddhism and Hinduism, but not Christianity. Or maybe we've come across the occasional quote attributed (often wrongly) to Christian mystics like Meister Eckhart or Julian of Norwich or Thomas Merton, so we think we've gotten the gist of the whole mysticism thing and either relegated it to inspirational memes or abandoned it as too dense and flowery and lofty— too mystical—to have any real place in our faith journey.

Yet mysticism really only means to follow the path of mystery. I daresay a relationship with God that has no interest in mystery is pitifully

---

1. See Carlyle, *On Heroes.*

limited. As G. K. Chesterton observed, "Mysticism keeps men sane. As long as you have mystery you have health; where you destroy mystery you create morbidity. . . . The whole secret of mysticism is this: that man can understand everything by the help of what he does not understand."[2] If this is the case, is it to our advantage—to our mental and spiritual and even physical health—that we write off the ideas of heroism and mysticism as having nothing much to do with us? Or could it be that a better understanding of mysticism and heroism will lead to a better understanding of God, our true selves, and as Chesterton said, everything?

We Can Be Heroes

It is with such questions in mind that I offer this book. If we can come to a better understanding of what it is to be a hero and what it is to be a mystic, then it's quite possible we might come to a better understanding of what it is to be ourselves. Perhaps our true self is located somewhere in a Venn diagram overlap of heroism and mysticism. This might especially be the case when we see how the two are connected, that the mystic journey to life with God is at the heart of the classic hero's journey of myth and legend, and vice versa. And we might be surprised to learn just how practical it all is, how much it has to do with our big questions: Is there more to life? Is there more to me? What is life's true treasure? What does it mean to be one with God, and what does that have to do with the mess and absurdities of the everyday world? These are some of the issues to be addressed on this mystical-heroic journey to life with God.

Our guide on this journey will be Flemish mystical theologian John of Ruusbroec (1293–1381). He is a favorite among scholars of mysticism, though the fact that the translation of his works into English was completed only in 2006 has kept him from being widely known. Still, writers like Evelyn Underhill and Thomas Merton considered him a genius and perhaps the greatest of medieval mystics. He's like one of those brilliant musicians who are mostly listened to only by other musicians. He's a mystic's mystic.

As such, Ruusbroec (ROOS-brook) will make a more than capable guide through our story, like one of Dante's guides in *The Divine Comedy* or like a Hogwarts professor. Wandering the streets of medieval Brussels, Belgium, too caught up in contemplative prayer to be aware of his ragged appearance, the humble priest might well have been recognizable as a

2. Chesterton, *Orthodoxy*, 22–23.

mystic. But a hero? Not very likely. Nevertheless, the turn his life would take and the journey to union with God that he would go on to narrate are unquestionably heroic. His unique brand of Christian mysticism, I am convinced, remains one of the most profound and relevant articulations of the way of purgation, illumination, union, and perfection in love. It is profound because it presents a life that, in its essential nature, is held in the embrace of the divine Unity. It is relevant because that same inwardly embraced life simultaneously moves outward in loving service to others with the divine Trinity. Fully contemplative and fully active, it is "the life that is truly life" (1 Tim 6:19). And it is where we will find the true self.

But we'll cover all of that in time. For now, suffice it to say it's all about life. Ruusbroec even orders his path of spiritual formation according to four *lives*: the Active Life, the Inner Life, the Contemplative Life, and the Common Life. Interestingly, these stages and many of their components align with the stages and tropes of the archetypal hero's journey found in myths and legends and sacred texts and folktales throughout history and around the world. I explore this connection more exhaustively elsewhere.[3] Here, however, we will take that research and learn to actually apply it to our own journey of spiritual formation. This is not merely an academic exercise or a theoretical supposition. This is life.

To that end, this book presents the complex and sometimes baffling teachings of mystical theology alongside the comparable stages of the hero's journey, a form we're likely familiar with from many of our favorite stories and films. The stages and tropes of the hero's journey were broadly analyzed and, to a certain degree, codified in the first half of the twentieth century by scholars like Russian literary theorist Vladimir Propp and American literature professor and mythologist Joseph Campbell. The characteristics of the hero's journey that they (and others) came to recognize are found in various kinds of stories across history and around the world.[4] Thus, the hero's journey is archetypal, which is to say it is a narrative structure that seems largely to transcend geo-sociocultural boundaries and represent a sort of metanarrative for the human experience.[5]

3. Pelfrey, *Spiritual Formation*.

4. Other scholars in the field include James George Frazer, Otto Rank, Richard Somerset Lord Raglan, Erich Auerbach, Claude Lévi-Strauss, Northrop Frye, René Girard, Dean Miller, Scott Allison and George Goethels, and others, most of whom had no choice but to build on (or, in some cases, around) the pioneering work of Propp and Campbell.

5. Patrick Hogan describes "archetypal patterns" as complexes of properties found across a wide range of literary works, extending back to ancient poems, stories, myths,

Though there are a number of minor stages and experiences, many of which will be touched on in this book, there are four major stages that will inform our journey:

1. The Call, which includes awakening and mentoring and departing for the journey

2. The Road, which includes initiation and the experience of trials in pursuit of an object of search

3. The Treasure, which is the person or thing or experience of value that is being pursued

4. The Return home to use the treasure and the journey's transformative lessons for the good of others

While equating formation in Christlikeness and union with God to the hero's journey might seem silly or even profane to some, a couple of things should be born in mind. First, myths and legends are not, at their core, fiction. In fact, they typically exist to relate deep truths that are too mysterious and profound—too *true*—to be easily systematized and explained on a more superficial or even intellectual level. And second, the hero's journey, at its core and in its origins, exists as the story of humanity's search for God. It is my position that the archetypal tropes and archetypal narrative patterns of the hero's journey are, in fact, *archetypal* because humans share an inherent relationship with God and, thus, are hardwired for the journey of divine union—the journey home—in which we find our true selves.

Therefore, this book is organized around the primary stages of the hero's journey. The first section is The Call, in which we are summoned to the adventure of life with God and we experience the initial aspects of the life of devotion, found in Ruusbroec's Active Life. The next section is The Road, in which we move past our familiar and controllable religiosity and into our deeper personhood, addressed in the first parts of Ruusbroec's Inner Life. The third section is The Treasure, in which we come to the deepest and highest states of union with God and formation in Godlikeness, seen in the rest of Ruusbroec's Inner Life and his Contemplative Life. The final section is The Return, in which all the stages and transformative lessons of the journey are integrated and employed in loving service to others, found in what Ruusbroec calls the Common Life.

and rituals. Archetypes are a central concept in the psychological theories of Carl Jung and the literary theories of Northrop Frye. Hogan, "Archetypal Patterns."

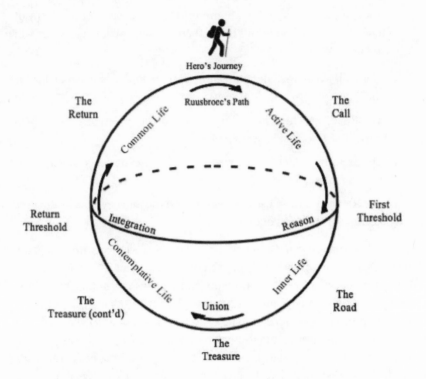

**A map of our quest: the stages of the hero's journey
and John of Ruusbroec's formational path**

Along the way, we will encounter the vivid imagery and metaphors that John of Ruusbroec and some other favorite mystics and teachers use to describe the ineffable process of union with God and perfection in God's love. There will be suggestions of spiritual practices to try that can help prepare us for that process, like a farmer prepares the land for fruitfulness. We will also encounter many of our favorite stories and characters as they help us better understand what it means to be a hero and a mystic. And hopefully, at some points along the way, we will encounter God and we will encounter ourselves—our true selves. And in the end, the greatest story of our lives will no longer remain an untold story.

Part I

THE CALL

1

The Story We're In

When Dorothy stood in the doorway and looked around, she could
see nothing but the great gray prairie on every side. Not a tree nor a
house broke the broad sweep of flat country that reached the edge of
the sky in all directions.

—L. Frank Baum, *The Wonderful Wizard of Oz*

*I*S THERE MORE TO LIFE *than this?* We've all had the thought. It might be
an expression of hopes and dreams, or it might be the result of exasperation and brokenness. But of all the things that people around the world and
across time have in common, this question is certainly one of the most
important. It comes to some in youth. Like the farm girl Dorothy Gale, in
The Wizard of Oz, dreaming of a life somewhere over the rainbow. Like
the farm boy, Luke Skywalker, in *Star Wars*, watching the setting suns and
longing for a life of meaning as part of a bigger cause. For others it comes
later in life. Like Tennyson's aging Ulysses, many journeys behind him, yet
still dreaming of newer worlds and determined to sail beyond the sunset.
Like Maya Angelou's generations upon generations—underestimated, dehumanized, trodden down yet rising again and again, like suns and moons
and tides . . . like hopes. Still I rise.

Is there more to life? For those who attend to the question, who are
willing to entertain it and nourish it and let it come to life, it becomes a Call.
A Call to Adventure of sorts. A Call to awaken to the adventure already
happening around us and within us might be more accurate. For it doesn't
usually come from out of nowhere. There might be a loss in our life or

the realization that something important is missing. It could be a sense of reeling in the years, feeling overcome by changes that occur in young adulthood or middle age. Or it might simply be the result of taking stock, of looking at life as a continuum and being underwhelmed by what lies behind, or what lies ahead, or both.

At this point there's good news and there's challenging news. The good news is that such thinking, whether born of the dreams of youth or the despair of age, is a wake-up Call. There is indeed more to life, far more than paying bills and trying to be nice and waiting to die. The challenging news is that the wake-up Call must be answered. Realizing that there is more is only the knock at the door. Opening the door, embracing what stands there, and following it out into the vast unknown is what comes next, and it is not for the uncommitted or faint of heart.

Meet Reverend John

In the 1330s in Belgium, a busy priest heard this Call and it awakened him to the promise of more to life. John of Ruusbroec was one of several priests serving in a glorious Gothic church in the growing metropolis of Brussels. When he was eleven, his poor single mother had sent him (it is also said that he ran away) from their small hometown to live with a wealthy relative in the city. This relative, a priest, saw to it that young John was given a first-class education, holy orders, and a fast track in the religious community. It was the makings of the classic story: poor country boy makes good in the big city.

However, despite his newfound stability and growing status, Reverend John (as he was called) was an unusual young man. He soaked himself in the Scriptures. He haunted the libraries, consuming volume after volume on theology and philosophy and the natural sciences. And he wandered the busy Brussels streets pondering what he read and caught up in prayerful ecstasy. He paid little attention to his appearance, and his shabbiness elicited both admiration and derision from passersby. Was he a pious holy man or a mad homeless man? (The line between the two is sometimes very thin.)

Reverend John eventually began working out his mystical theology in writing. His first book, *The Realm of Lovers*, was that sort of theological exercise. He intended it for only himself and a few close associates, but much later he discovered it had been copied and shared widely. (He discovered this when he traveled to teach a group of monks and found that they had a copy of his unpublished book. Yet the gracious priest declined the monks' offer to return the bootlegged writings. He even wrote another work—*The Little Book of Enlightenment*—to help clarify some issues they were struggling with in the bootlegged book!) In his second book, *The Spiritual Espousals*, he developed his ideas more fully and presented them publicly in a refined and dynamic narrative. It was a hit. Reverend John was gaining a following even beyond bustling Brussels. But the growing acclaim left the mystic wanting . . . less. Or rather, wanting more by way of less.

Even as his mystical writings began to be circulated and to attract a considerable following, Reverend John knew the only way to get more out of his life was to let go. His life needed refining and focus—simplicity. He had established a small contemplative group including his benefactor uncle and another clergy friend. They studied and worshiped and prayed together, yet they remained unsettled. Finally, Ruusbroec and his companions asked permission to relocate to an abandoned hermitage in the Sonian Forest a few miles outside Brussels, near the small town of Groenendaal (Green Valley). The bishop did not exactly refuse, but he would grant the request only if the trio agreed to establish a chapel and a house for at least five more monks.

So, like the desert fathers and mothers before them, the small band left the safety of the city walls to follow God into the unprotected wild. It was Easter of 1343. They built the chapel and house and, within a few years, adopted the Rule of St. Augustine and obtained official church status as an Augustinian monastery. The middle-aged Reverend John had found his home. For nearly forty more years he helped order the life of his Groenendaal community. He traveled many miles on foot—even well into old age—to meet with anyone who wished to know more about his teachings. And he regularly slipped away into his beloved forest to meditate and to write about the way of perfect loving union with God, about the heroic adventure of living the life God is living. It was a story that had to be told, and John of Ruusbroec told it the rest of his long life.

The Bridegroom Cometh: A Mystical Earworm

"The kingdom of heaven," says Jesus, "is like ten bridesmaids who took their lamps and went to meet the bridegroom. Five of them were foolish and didn't take any oil for their lamps. Five were wise and did take flasks of oil. As the groom was delayed, they all got sleepy and drifted off. Then, at midnight, a call was heard: 'See, the bridegroom comes! Go out to meet him!' The bridesmaids shot up and scrambled to light their lamps. The foolish ones begged the wise ones for some oil, but the wise were worried they wouldn't have enough. So, while the unprepared bridesmaids went into town to buy oil, the bridegroom came. Everyone went with him to the wedding feast, and the door was shut behind them. The five foolish bridesmaids finally got to the party and banged on the door, but the doorkeeper didn't know them and sent them away.

"So wake up!" Jesus concludes. "Keep oil in your lamp. Watch for the coming of the bridegroom and his kingdom" (Matt 25:1–13, my paraphrase).

Jesus often ends his stories with a Call to wake up and watch out. In fact, much of Jesus's earthly ministry could be considered one big wake-up Call. He spent his life waking the world to the fact that the kingdom of God's loving, governing presence has come to earth and is available to any and all who want it. But the world is so full of temptations and distractions that only those who listen for the Call and watch for the coming will be ready to go out on the kingdom journey.

In this story—Jesus's Parable of the Wise and Foolish Bridesmaids—John of Ruusbroec found a structure for his masterwork, *The Spiritual Espousals*. Like a song lyric you can't get out of your head, over and over Reverend John uses the refrain, "See, the bridegroom comes! Go out to meet him!" He breaks it down into four elements: 1) see; 2) the bridegroom comes; 3) go out; 4) to meet him. This mystical earworm is a really important motif for his teaching, so we do well to get it stuck in our heads too. The "espousal" (i.e., marriage) in his book's title refers to the union of us in our human nature with God in God's divine nature as Unity and Trinity. It is a marriage between the devoted seeker as the bride and Christ as the Bridegroom. And that "midnight cry" motif—our mystical earworm—is a Call to transformation, to the journey of union with God, and to a great and holy adventure. It is a Call to getting more out of life: See, the bridegroom comes! Go out to meet him!

Our Initial Situation

The first leg of the journey is what Reverend John calls the Active Life. This stage focuses on outward virtues and loving activity. However, that is not why it is called the Active Life, because such activities and virtues will

continue through all the stages of the journey. It is active because these virtues require greater effort on the part of the sojourning seeker than should
be required at later stages. It requires an active leaving behind of life and
the world as we've known them. This is the stage of hearing the Call, of
gathering oil for the lamp and trimming the wick. It might even be the stage
of considering if the journey is worth the effort and possibly refusing that
Call. This is because of competition and distractions from the world around
us and the noise within us.

The Call—the knock at life's door—comes in our everyday lives in
the everyday world. It's what Vladimir Propp calls the "initial situation"
of the hero's journey.[1] It's the story we are already in, the inner and outer
circumstances that have us longing for more. According to Propp, one very
common story line in folktales is that the would-be hero lacks a bride and
sets out to find true love.[2] This can be a larger quest that includes finding
love, but more often it is a quest for a specific lover who has gone missing.
In many ways this is exactly the story Ruusbroec tells, the story he would
say we are all being called to live: the adventure of being united with our
true Love. And only in union with our true Love will we find our true self.

The story we find ourselves in, says Reverend John, is about separation
from God. We were made in original blessedness, made to be united with
God and with each other and with the natural world. Yet we've become
exiled to an island of sinful alienation, an exile largely of our own making.
Despite being made according to God's own image and set on the path to
grow in God's likeness and to enjoy God's company, we repeatedly give in
to the ancient temptation of the serpent: to become like God, but to do so
without God (Gen 3:4–5). It is the old lie that still haunts and hounds us
today. Cutting ourselves off from God winds up cutting us off from each
other, from the natural world, and from our true selves.

But that's not the end of our story. Within our exile, the second Person
of the Trinity, God the Son, has come to bring us home to God's kingdom
and company. This Son is the true Image of God, and in his incarnation as
Jesus of Nazareth we find the truest and fullest marriage of humanity and
divinity. In him we find the way of union, of living as one with God and
each other and all God has made. As Jesus puts it in his homespun way: "I
am the vine; you are the branches. If you remain in me and I in you, you
will bear much fruit. . . . As the Father has loved me, so have I loved you.

1. Propp, *Morphology of the Folktale*, 25.
2. Propp, *Morphology of the Folktake*, 35.

Now live in my love" (John 15:5, 9). In Christ, God has visited us in our alienation, shown us God's way of love, striven as a champion against our enemies of sin and death, broken down our prisons and won our struggles, and put to death our death by his death. Beyond our positive or negative feelings toward Christianity as a religion, we must admit it's a rather powerful story.

And that's one of Ruusbroec's great lines, that Christ has "put to death our death by his death."[3] It's the foundation for getting more out of life. Jesus himself said that he came so that we could have life—and not just life, but full and abundant life (John 10:10). But like so many others, his message of life was answered with death. There are many thoughts and theories regarding the mystery of the crucifixion of Jesus of Nazareth and what exactly was happening in Christ's death, most of which are beyond the scope of this book. One aspect that is relevant for us here, however, is that Jesus exposed the bankruptcy, futility, and evil of humanity's notions of power through killing, self-aggrandizement, control, and violence. He was ground to death by the gears of human power and empire and then was raised to life on the other side, demonstrating the absurdity of the whole enterprise. As Peter would summarize soon after the events, "You killed the author of life, but God raised him from the dead" (Acts 3:15). Killing the author of life—it's an image that speaks volumes. But God raising him is the last word.

At one point, right after Jesus's gruesome execution and subsequent entombment, some of the women come to prepare his body so that it can decay properly, and then his bones will be collected into a box and given to his relatives, in keeping with custom. But the women are intercepted by messengers from God who proclaim that Jesus, who was very much dead, is now very much alive. They ask the women the very pointed, loaded question: "Why do you look for the living among the dead?" (Luke 24:5).

This, essentially, is another way of addressing our question: Is there more to life? Christ has put to death our death by his death, so that we might rise with his rising to life. So why do we keep haunting graveyards, looking for life among the tombs? We keep stumbling over those same bankrupt cultural graves: violence, manipulation, empire, prejudice, greed, oppression, and so many other expressions of our collective fear.

But we also trip over graves of a more personal nature, believing the old lie that one of them will surely make us more godlike over our lives and

---

3. John of Ruusbroec, *Spiritual Espousals*, a26–27 (part 1 [a], lines 26–27, and so throughout).

our little slice of the world: A different job. A different partner. A different place with different people. Travel, a change of clothes, a leaner body, a fatter paycheck, a better house, a bigger following, and more influence. Perhaps one or two such things will help us, though they quite possibly will hurt us or even kill us, especially when they are an expression of the false self. These are not the more we're looking for. Not one of these things is what's knocking on the door of our life.

Divine Sight: Awakening to the Journey

See, the bridegroom comes! Go out to meet him! This is the stuff of the heroic journey of real life, of abundant life, of God life. The invitation is not to a greater realization of material wealth and worldly success. That is far too small a life. Instead, the invitation is to share in the very life of God. That is a life that touches all of earth and reaches into the heart of heaven. As C. S. Lewis wrote, "Aim at Heaven and you will get earth 'thrown in': aim at earth and you will get neither."[4] This is eternal life, "the life that is truly life" (1 Tim 6:19), which does not simply mean unending life (though that is a characteristic) but the life of God and with God. This is our quest, the untold story of our true self. And it begins right where we are and right as we are.

Within Jesus's Call to the adventure of eternal life—our "mystical earworm"—are a divine double instruction and a divine double promise. It's the key to what we should do and what we will attain. See (instruction); the bridegroom comes (promise); go out (instruction); to meet him (promise). Our part is to see and to go out. God's part is to come and to unite with us. As we will come to understand, however, God is at work in all of it. There is no part of the load that we carry alone.

See. We are instructed that we need to learn to see. But when we look around, all we see is life and the world as we've always known them. We might even focus on what is missing from our lives, the thing that makes us feel like life is less than it should be. We are like Dorothy surveying the empty plains around her and the longing within her. However, as Reverend John explains, the path of the eternal adventure begins with no longer settling for natural sight, for seeing things as we've always looked at them. Rather, we must begin to see supernaturally. And to see supernaturally, we need three things.

4. Lewis, *Mere Christianity*, 134.

The first thing needed in order to truly see is light, specifically *the light of God's grace*. We likely think of grace in terms of unmerited favor, something like God's goodness and love at work in our lives and for our sakes, not because of our worthiness, but because of God's good and loving nature. And that is accurate. But it might not have crossed our minds to think of grace as something that is ongoing, and to see grace in rather utilitarian terms as light that we use to walk the path to union with God. Grace is like a lantern, which is lit and given to us by God, but which we must carry and aim.

Reverend John breaks it down even further into God's grace given in two ways: *prevenient* grace and *meritorious* grace. God's prevenient grace (literally "grace that comes before") is God's good and loving action within and around *all* people, calling everyone to share in God's life. God's prevenient grace acts as a herald sounding the Call to the eternal adventure. This grace takes many forms, both positive and seemingly negative, in the world and in an individual's life. We might experience a loss or a gain, an illness or a healing, the conviction for our own sins or inspiration from the holy life of Jesus and others, or any number of other small or great inner or outer moments that serve to draw our hearts and minds to God. Additionally, as we will come to better understand later, every one of us is hardwired for this journey, in part because of a fundamental inclination toward God called the "spark of the soul," which Ruusbroec describes as "the soul's natural tendency toward its source."[5]

Each instance of prevenient grace is a knock on life's door, and the result is a crisis: Are we going to answer the Call and go on the journey? Or are we going to lock the door and settle back into life as we know it and think we can control it? It's Neo's crisis in *The Matrix*: take the red pill and wake up to reality, or take the blue pill and go back to the blissful ignorance of illusory life in the Matrix. And to be sure, the blue pill is a very real option. A refusal of the Call is not unusual. When Obi-Wan Kenobi tells Luke Skywalker they must answer Princess Leia's call for help, the boy refuses and insists he must go back to the farm and help his uncle with the harvest. In *The Lion King*, Simba spends years avoiding confronting his uncle over the murder of his father and taking his rightful place as heir. The respected Jewish teacher and leader Nicodemus refuses Jesus's initial call to be born again, exclaiming, "How can this be?" (John 3:8). But later he

---

5. John of Ruusbroec, *Mirror of Eternal Blessedness*, l. 892.

is found defending Jesus (7:50–51) and then caring for Jesus's lifeless body and preparing it for burial (19:39).

Many if not most people who answer the Call only do so after an initial refusal, sometimes several refusals. However, to stop with a refusal of the Call is ultimately to make oneself one's god. In this case, as Joseph Campbell explains, "God himself, the will of God, the power that would destroy one's egocentric system, becomes a monster."[6] This is to settle for the lie of becoming Godlike without the participation of God. But the light of prevenient grace must eventually be followed if we are to come to the other, even greater light: meritorious grace.

God's meritorious grace is God's work by which we *merit* eternal life, that is to say, by which we participate in the redeeming love and transforming life of God. Many have been exposed to the idea of meritorious grace in terms of "getting saved." Sadly, this interpretation has been reduced to something like a one-and-done act of walking an aisle and "making a decision for Christ" that doesn't require anything more of us and may or may not make much difference afterward. This is akin to thinking of "getting married" as only what happens on the wedding day.

Instead, meritorious grace is the second part of the aforementioned story, in which the incarnate God visits us in our exile and makes the way for us to come into a new life of oneness. John Wesley (1703–91) offers a helpful picture of this process in terms of a house, with repentance as the porch, faith as the door, and holiness as the house itself.[7] So here, prevenient grace (Wesley calls it "preventing grace") is our Call and desire to come home, and meritorious grace ("justifying grace") is stepping up onto the porch and walking through the door with the faith that this truly is home. The rest of the journey is about fully moving in and learning to live in the house of holiness with God. Ultimately, it really is all about hearing the parental Call and coming home to a new life.

Ruusbroec describes this meritorious grace as "the inworking of God in the soul above time."[8] It's an eternal matter taking place in the essence of our life. As we'll learn, our life is eternally bound up with God's life. So, coming to see supernaturally must be God's work, not ours, for we cannot merit or earn this new way of being. It is Christ alone whose life and death and resurrection accomplished it. Remember, he "put to death our death

6. Campbell, *Hero with Thousand Faces*, 49–50.
7. Wesley, "Principles of a Methodist," 227.
8. John of Ruusbroec, *Spiritual Espousals*, a121.

by his death," and he did so solely because of his love, mercy, and grace. Beyond the many theories surrounding Christ's crucifixion and death, we look to Christ crucified and resurrected and ascended and find God showing us a better way, the way by which we might leave the graveyards behind and follow him on the path of life.

So, God lights the lantern for this new path, but we must choose to see by it. Therefore, for those who desire to be "in Christ" (as Paul called this new way of being, see Rom 8:1), the light of God's prevenient and meritorious grace has entered the soul like the golden rays of the morning sun coming through a window. A new day has dawned!

Moving on . . . our response to God's grace must be the second step in learning to see supernaturally: *a God-turned will*. This is the movement of stepping up onto God's porch and walking through God's door because, yes, we want to live with God. This is an exercise of free will, the decisive act of truly answering the Call. Neo swallows the red pill. Luke leaves the dirt farm behind and takes off with Obi-Wan. We decide that we want what God wants, for God's way to become our way. We respond to the supernatural light of God's grace by directing the free will of our lives toward God and God's will for us. We say to God, "We're in this together!" And God says to us (has always been saying to us), "Yes, we're in this together!"

The result is what Reverend John calls a "love-bond," which is the uniting of God's will for us and our will for God. Each is incomplete without the other. Emerging from this love-bond is the third aspect of supernatural sight: *a pure conscience*. What this pure conscience looks like inwardly is a resolve to leave behind the ways of sin and death—the cultural and personal graveyards—and to commit to walk with God in humble obedience toward life. Outwardly, the pure conscience is manifested in virtues and good works. Essentially, it's all just a big "Yes!" to God's big "Yes!" to us.

So, these three—the light of God's grace, a God-turned will, and a pure conscience—form what Ruusbroec calls "a divine way of seeing."[9] Our eyes are beginning to open to God's way of seeing and being. John Wesley offers an interesting description of this awakening and enlightenment, expanding on the description of faith in Heb 11:1 as "the assurance of things unseen":

> We have a prospect of the invisible things of God; we see the *spiritual world*, which is all round about us, and yet no more discerned by our natural faculties than if it had not being; and we see the *eternal world*, piercing through the veil which hangs between time

9. John of Ruusbroec, *Spiritual Espousals*, a149.

and eternity. Clouds and darkness then rest upon it no more, but we already see the glory which shall be revealed.[10]

We see the spiritual world all round about us. We see the eternal world piercing through the veil. This is an awareness that there is, indeed, more to life. It is an awakening to the reality that God is alive and at work within us and around us, knocking at the door of our lives and urging us to come along. It is a glimpse of the path of the eternal adventure opening before us.

And yet, this is only the beginning. We have merely accepted the invitation, said yes to the journey, decided that we do want to tell the story of our true self. However, if we are to go on this quest, we will need a helper.

Way-Stop #1: Reflection

Each chapter of this book will end at a Way-Stop where we will pause to reflect, assess, and get our bearings. As we undertake this journey and explore its territories it is important to look closely and honestly at our own story. We must keep what we are learning from becoming a cold or trivial or maybe entertaining lesson in the heroic and mystic way, and instead recognize how such things are unfolding in our own lives. For one thing, it is not always exciting and might never strike us as much of an adventure. We can recall, for example, how Mother Teresa of Calcutta admitted to many long years of spiritual dryness with no tangible awareness of God's presence, even as she lived as a striking example of heroism, as divine light and color in the "great gray prairie" of the world.

Perhaps we, too, know such dryness and grayness. Maybe we started the journey eagerly and faithfully at one point but were disappointed—by circumstances or an event, by a person or group, by the church or our brand of faith, by God, by life in general. Maybe we're stuck wondering if there really is more to life. We're not yet ready to open the door and set out into the unknown. We're scared of what we might find, or that there's nothing to be found at all. Or perhaps we've never heard the knock, never entertained the notion that God could be calling us to share in God's own life and all that that might mean. If that is the case, maybe this is the moment. *Knock, knock* . . .

On the other hand, maybe it's all very exciting! We are finding ourselves one way or another in this opening stage of the journey: the Call to

10. Wesley, "Scripture Way of Salvation," 2.1 (pp. 442–43; emphases original).

something different and the Active Life of virtues and loving activity. We are beginning to "See" in a new, supernatural way. We are learning the practice of submission, by which we begin to surrender our personal salvation projects—money, pleasure, approval, control—to God's life transforming ours.

Whatever the case, a practice we might try is filling the day (morning, bedtime, throughout) with some form of the prayer of Thomas à Kempis (ca. 1380–1471) from *The Imitation of Christ*: "Lord, you know what is best. Give what you will, as you will, when you will. Do with me as you know best."[11] We then look for opportunities throughout the day to practice this surrender, letting our old ways serve as reminders to see and behave in new and different ways. But it must be *our* ways, *our* life that we bring into the story. God calls us where we are and as we are. It does us no good to play games or to pretend to be someone else. You are seeking your own true self, after all, not someone else's.

So, with authenticity, receptivity, humility, and a bit of courage, we can begin to leave behind life and the world as we have known them and to step through the door to a new way of being. But first, help is on the way.

Bearings

- *Location*: the Call > the Active Life > "See"

- *Key Concepts*: the Call to Adventure; initial situation; the Active Life; prevenient grace; spark of the soul; meritorious grace; God-turned will; love-bond; pure conscience; divine way of seeing

- *Practice*: prayer of surrender; practicing surrender

11. Thomas à Kempis, *Imitation of Christ*, 3.15.2.

2

THE HELPER WE'VE ALWAYS WANTED

Telemachus, your father was such an old friend of mine that I will find
you a ship and will come with you myself. . . . There are many ships in
Ithaca both old and new; I will run my eye over them for you and will
choose the best; we will get her ready and will put out to sea without
delay.

—Homer, *The Odyssey*

W E AREN'T MEANT TO go it alone. We can't. No matter how independent we think we are, our lives are marked by protectors, teachers, providers, and guides. True heroes are no different. We often think
of the romantic ideal of the loner hero, the "superman" (*Übermensch*) of
Nietzsche, in need of no one (especially not God) and nothing but one's
own limitless potential.[1] But brooding, self-important introspection is not
the stuff of genuine transformation. The truly heroic journey requires a
helper, an aid. A would-be hero needs a "mentor," which actually comes
from the character Mentor who, in Homer's *Odyssey*, was Odysseus's friend
and adviser whom he asked to watch over his son, Telemachus, and who
sometimes was the goddess Athena in disguise.

Like Mentor, the helper might be divine and/or supernatural, or at
least possess such qualities. It is Obi-Wan Kenobi and Yoda teaching Luke

---

1. In some cases, the idea of the *Übermensch* as a class of human with extraordinary
traits and potential has resulted in Nazism and other expressions of superiority, ethnic or
otherwise. This, in very many ways, is the exact opposite of the sort of hero the present
book has in mind.

15

Skywalker the ways of the Force. It is Glinda the Good giving Dorothy the magic slippers and directing her to Emerald City. It is Gandalf the Grey, Mary Poppins, Charles Xavier, Albus Dumbledore, and Fairy Godmother. And don't we all want such a person in our lives, imparting wisdom, skills, guidance, and maybe even a magical gift or supernatural powers?

But who? Perhaps we've been blessed with a mentoring relationship or two in our life—a parent or sibling, a teacher or coach, a religious or community leader. Maybe they've lived up to or even surpassed our expectations, or maybe they've disappointed us. But no matter how meaningful the relationship might have been, there's one mentor who is uniquely qualified for our present journey. And yet, in our longings for a wise and skilled helper who can guard us and guide us in both our day-to-day life and our big-picture journey, it seems this same figure often fails to make most wish lists.

That figure, of course, is Jesus. Sure, plenty of people—religious and nonreligious alike—would cite Jesus as an important teacher, maybe the most important. Some even consider him the divine Son of God and Savior of the world. But within the belief systems of both the "good teacher" and the "divine Savior" crowds there often remains a very significant empty spot.

The problem with many Christians in this area is they get so concerned about the people who view Jesus as *only* a wise teacher, they resist the truth that, yes, Jesus was in fact a wise teacher. Instead, these Christians tend to go right from Jesus's virgin birth to his crucifixion and resurrection, skipping all the stuff in the middle. They are so defensive about Christ's divinity and death that they downplay his humanity and life. Even the Apostles' Creed does it: "He was conceived by the Holy Spirit, born of the virgin Mary, suffered under Pontius Pilate, was crucified." It jumps right from his first breath to his final hours. Wasn't there anything between "born" and "suffered" that matters? There's a whole significant period of Jesus's life there that was filled with teaching and interacting with people and training followers, many of whom actually called him "teacher." This gap usually comes from an altruistic place of wanting to emphasize what people see as the urgent message of Jesus's saving death and resurrection, but the result is a very narrow and incomplete understanding of salvation, and of Jesus.

What is missing is what Dallas Willard calls the "great *omission*" from Jesus's Great Commission.[2] As Willard observes, many people tend to think

2. See Willard, *Great Omission*, ix–xiv.

of Jesus's closing words in Matthew (the Great Commission) like this: "All authority in heaven and on earth has been given to me. Therefore go and make disciples of all nations, baptizing them in the name of the Father and of the Son and of the Holy Spirit. And surely I am with you always, to the very end of the age" (Matt 28:18–20). Is that right? It seems right, but it isn't. What is often omitted, certainly in practice if not also in word, are Jesus's crucial instructions regarding discipleship: "baptizing them in the name of the Father and of the Son and of the Holy Spirit, *and teaching them to obey everything I have commanded you*" (v. 20). The resurrected Jesus is essentially saying, "Go back and learn and live and share all that stuff I taught you after I was born and before I was crucified."

Considering Jesus's claim of all authority in heaven and on earth, his expectation that we will learn and practice everything he taught, and his promise that he is with us in each moment and every epoch of human existence, it sounds very much like Jesus wants to be that helper to us that we've so longed for. We see it in the Gospels when Jesus calls his disciples. It is never a call to go find some random adventure or self-guided spirituality. In his real and earthy way, Jesus encounters people at work and in the marketplace and says, "Come, follow me" (e.g., Mark 1:16–18; John 1:43–50). And Jesus's Call to Adventure is never "Accept me into your heart and you'll go to heaven when you die." Instead, Jesus's Call is "Come be my apprentice and learn my teaching and you will know the truth, and the truth will make you free" (John 8:31).

And that's exactly how Reverend John sees it, explaining that though God might seem hidden from us, we are not hidden from God.[3] Like Jesus spying potential disciples in their everyday doings, God sees and knows us and wants us to see and know God. And God has given us God's own mirror and image in God the Son, incarnated as Jesus of Nazareth, the Wisdom of God and our sought-after Bridegroom.

In short: God looks like Jesus. God doesn't *only* look like Jesus, as we'll come to better understand along the way of our journey. But we do ourselves a huge favor if we'll settle in and try taking him at his word: "Anyone who has seen me has seen the Father" (John 14:9). If we want a wise and powerful mentor and helper, and one who just happens to have been given all authority in heaven and on earth, then we should commit ourselves to learn and practice the way of Jesus.

---

3. See John of Ruusbroec, *Mirror of Eternal Blessedness*, ll. 240–44.

Wax On/Wax Off and the Way, Truth, and Life

One of the most beloved helper characters in popular culture is Mr. Miyagi from *The Karate Kid*, memorably portrayed by Noriyuki "Pat" Morita alongside Ralph Macchio's hero character, Daniel LaRusso. Having recently moved from New Jersey to California, Daniel is alone and struggling with alienation and bullying in his new surroundings. In his building's maintenance man, Mr. Miyagi, Daniel finds a sympathetic defender who teaches him the ways of both karate and friendship.

One of the most memorable sequences in the original film (second only to the final battle and the famous "crane kick") is Mr. Miyagi's method of training young Daniel, consisting of a series of chores. Daniel washes and waxes Miyagi's many classic cars. He sands the wooden deck that extends all around Miyagi's large backyard. He stains Miyagi's extensive fence (both sides!). He paints Miyagi's house. Each chore must be done in a very specific manner, and always accompanied by attentive breathing—in through the nose, out through the mouth.

Finally, having done these chores day after day, a broken and exasperated Daniel explodes at his teacher, complaining that he has learned nothing from him but servile labor. But then the genius of the Miyagi method is revealed: the repeated motions of Daniel's grueling daily chores have been teaching him fundamental karate moves all along, moves that are now so ingrained that they are second nature. Karate, it turns out, is in everything—from breathing, to waxing the car and painting the house, to relationships.

The Ruusbroec method of spiritual formation is similar. It sees Christ at work in all areas of life—from Jesus's incarnation and redeeming work accomplished in the past, to his activity in our lives and the church and the world in the present, to his future judgment and everlasting reign. For Reverend John, Christ is both the object of our quest and the means of reaching that object. As Jesus himself said, "I am the way and the truth and the life" (John 14:6). His is the true way *of* being, and he is the true way *to* that way of being. (If it's a mystical teacher we want, we need look no further!) For this journey of divine union, we are on our way to Christ as Bridegroom, and we are accompanied and empowered along the way by Christ as Helper, Teacher, and Mentor. For Daniel LaRusso, it would be as if Mr. Miyagi *is* karate. Watch him, follow him, and Daniel will become karate too. That's the way Reverend John presents Christ as Helper, and he does so according to three advents or "comings" of Christ.

Reverend John's Dojo: The Three Comings of Christ

The Bridegroom Comes. We'll recall that Ruusbroec is making use of Jesus's parable and mystical earworm: "See, the bridegroom comes! Go out to meet him!" We discussed what it means to "See" in the previous chapter, awakening to God's reality and Call to the adventure of divine union and Godlikeness. Now we'll consider what it is that we are to see, namely the coming of the Bridegroom. In this first leg of the journey, the Active Life, Christ the Bridegroom comes as our Helper for the journey. And the *first coming of Christ* was in his incarnation in time and space, in first-century Palestine, in which we find what Reverend John calls three roots of virtue and perfection. We might think of these as three banners hanging in Reverend John's dojo, indicating the three foundational rules of the Jesus Way.

The first foundational rule of virtue in Christ's first coming is *humility*. Within the very fact of the incarnation we see God the Son humbling himself to become human (see Phil 2:5–11), followed by the humility of his birth into poverty and his life of service and submission. So we must likewise be humble.

The second foundational rule of virtue in Christ's first coming is *charity* (i.e., active love). Charity is the origin and source of all virtues, and it is seen especially in Christ's life of benevolence and faithfulness in caring for the needs of others. For anyone who asked of him, Jesus fed them and healed them, both physically and spiritually, drawing from the inexhaustible riches of the Holy Spirit and his own divinity and humanity. So we must likewise be charitable.

And the third foundational rule of virtue seen in Christ's first coming is *patient endurance in suffering.* For this, Reverend John recounts examples across the span of Jesus's earthly life—from his birth in poverty, to his fasting and temptation, to his itinerant preaching and confrontations with religious leaders, and finally, in his passion and crucifixion. This is our model, and so we should likewise be faithful and patient in enduring life's challenges and suffering.

Therefore, any student of the Ruusbroec Method of the Jesus Way must carefully examine and imitate the lessons of humility, charity, and patient endurance found in the first coming of Christ in the incarnation. These are the foundational rules, the roots of virtue and perfection. In short: read the Gospels, know the Gospels, live the Gospels.

The second coming of Christ is typically thought of as the Lord's final return to judge the world in the future or to rapture believers away from the earth, which is an erroneous and unbiblical teaching.[4] Reverend John, however, speaks of Christ's second coming in terms of the present. This is Christ the Helper's daily presence, blessing us and empowering us with grace and new gifts and virtues. The God we see in Jesus is the living God, not a dead figure whose followers jotted down his sayings and practices for historic preservation. Instead, he is alive and active in the world, in our lives, and in our training. This is an especially remarkable aspect of the Ruusbroec Method.

Reverend John paints a picture of this dynamic relationship as the sun shining in a valley between two mountains. Christ, "the sun of righteousness" (Mal 4:2), stands in his zenith at the right hand of the Father (the place of authority) and shines his light into the valley of humility, which is created by a humble heart acknowledging its need for God. On either side are the two mountains of desire: one, to serve and praise God in worship; and the other, to obtain virtues and noble character. The divine light reflects off of these mountains into the valley of the humble heart, which becomes brighter and more illuminated by grace, warmed in charity, and fruitful in virtues and good works.

Reverend John also includes participation in the community and sacraments of the faithful as vital for experiencing this present and ongoing second coming of Christ, who said, "Where two or three gather in my name, there am I with them" (Matt 18:20).

Finally, *the third coming of Christ* is in the future, considered in terms of both the hour of our death and the final judgment of all. At this point, we (individually and collectively) must relinquish time and appear in God's presence, must give an account of our words and deeds, and must receive Christ's ultimate wisdom and right judgment on all matters. Despite negative and misguided attitudes about the notion of divine judgment, we should embrace it as a good thing, as the decisive action by which all that is wrong is finally set right by the good God who is Wisdom and Love. The anticipation of Christ's third coming in the future should inform our daily lives in the present through an attitude and actions in keeping with God's loving presence, God's goodness and mercy, and God's justice and power.

So, finally, if we are setting out to walk the path to the treasure of our true self as one with God, we must look to Christ as our Helper: the Christ

---

4. The Bible's reference to rapture (lit. "to be caught up") is 1 Thess 4:17, a passage about the general resurrection. The purpose of believers being "caught up" is to join Christ in his return to earth. It's about the Lord's coming (14–15), not believers leaving.

of history and the Gospels; the Christ who is "with you always" (Matt 28:20) in each present, powerful, pregnant moment; and the Christ of eternity, to whom "all authority in heaven and on earth has been given" (Matt 28:18). The mentor, the teacher, the master we've longed for has been with us all along. He shows up every day for any student who will also show up to learn from him the way of full life with God. Christ has come, is coming, and will forever come to be *both* our relentless Savior *and* our loving Lord. However, in order to experience the fullness of his salvation, we must go out to him.

At School in the Kingdom of the Soul

Go out. The three comings of Christ ("the Bridegroom comes") must be met by our active response ("go out"). When Mr. Miyagi asks Daniel if he is ready to begin training, Daniel replies, "I guess so." The teacher immediately offers his would-be student a crucial lesson: If you walk on the left side of the road or on the right side, you're safe. If you walk in the middle of the road, sooner or later a car will come along and you'll get squished like a grape. It's the same with karate, he continues. Karate "yes" or karate "no"—safe. Karate "guess so," sooner or later you'll get squished like a grape.

Tragically, there are many "guess so" Christians. Follow Jesus "yes" or follow Jesus "no" are legitimate choices. Follow Jesus "guess so" is not an option he leaves open for us. As he said plainly, "Why do you call me, 'Lord, Lord,' and do not do what I say?" (Luke 6:46). The idea of believing in Jesus as one's Savior and calling him Lord without then actually learning from him and following him is nonsensical to Jesus. For him, salvation is far more about life than about death.

And yet, countless middle-of-the-road Christians have done considerable harm not only to themselves but also to the witness of Christ throughout the world by espousing such "cheap grace," as Dietrich Bonhoeffer called it.[5] Bonhoeffer watched numerous "guess so" Christians slip their middle-of-the-road faith comfortably into Nazism. And still today, "guess so" Christians by the millions continue to water down the faith with all manner of -isms. Perhaps we're too afraid of seeming judge-y to recognize and decry what John Wesley called "the almost Christian." Or maybe we're afraid it's us. Whatever the case, the choice is crucial: yes or no to

---

5. Bonhoeffer, *Cost of Discipleship*, 43–56.

Christ. We must be committed to go out as often as the Bridegroom comes, to show up for Christ the same way he shows up for us. No more "guess so."

With that, the training sequence begins. The teacher works alongside the student, who sweats and struggles through workouts, runs in the cold and rain or burns the midnight oil in the library or the lab, fails again and again to the point of giving up all hope. Finally, with the teacher's guiding insistence and belief in the student, failures begin to give way to little successes, retreat and defeat open up to a horizon of potential victory. But all of this can happen only if the student, the would-be hero, shows up.

According to the Ruusbroec Method, our going out is directed toward God, toward ourselves, and toward our neighbors (which include animals and the natural world). And what this going out looks like is *justice* and *charity*, with a spirit of *humility*. The example Christ gives is always to strive upward toward the kingdom of God (Matt 6:33), which Ruusbroec says is God himself.[6] God is the source of charity, and it flows from God and dwells in God by the act of uniting us with God. (Now watch this . . .)

Reverend John explains that justice arises from charity in an effort "to perfect all conduct and all virtues that are honorable and befitting to *the kingdom of God, that is, the soul*."[7] Do we see what happened? Reverend John has moved from saying that the kingdom of God is God himself, to now saying that the kingdom of God is our own soul. This seems to be the result of that "act of uniting" us with God, so that the kingdom of God that *is* God enters into us, thus making *us*—our soul (the essence of our aliveness)—God's kingdom. This is a crucial understanding of reality and the true self: the kingdom of God is not fundamentally external to us but is in our own soul, the result of God's indwelling, though it will be expressed and bear fruit externally. Reverend John calls this, appropriately, *the kingdom of the soul*.

Our mystic guide develops this image of the kingdom of the soul in detail, using it to present the virtues that should characterize a life of "going out," of showing up for Christ the Helper and his training. Essentially, this section is all about character formation. Ruusbroec uses the word "nobility," which is appropriate since what we're talking about is becoming the kind of person who flourishes as a citizen, a noble, of God's kingdom. The foundation of the kingdom is charity, justice, and humility—these are the essentials. He explains that charity holds a person before God's fathomless

6. See John of Ruusbroec, *Spiritual Espousals*, a411.

7. John of Ruusbroec, *Spiritual Espousals*, a414 (emphasis added).

goodness, justice before God's eternal truth, and humility before God's sublime majesty.

So, we get a picture of God and, at the same time, a picture of who we're being formed to be: God's goodness is limitless, so this should drive us to be charitable (actively loving) to all; God's truth is eternal, so this should drive us to be just and to work for justice; God's majesty is sublime, so we should respond by being humble. And all of this is the foundation upon which the virtuous life is built. The result of drilling our life down into this foundation is the eradication of our pride and the sin that emerges from it. Hardly a small matter!

Next, Ruusbroec proceeds to build on the foundation, presenting some key virtues of the kingdom of the soul:

- ❧ obedience and submission of our will

- ❧ patience

- ❧ meekness and mercifulness

- ❧ compassion and shared suffering

- ❧ generosity

- ❧ moderation and temperance inside and out

- ❧ purity of soul and of body

This is quite a list, and it is in the middle of numerous rapid-fire attributes and lessons and images (with more to come!). Therefore, it is vital that we proceed slowly and consider all of these lessons thoughtfully and deeply. We might do well to journal about some of these or address them in some creative way or another, to assess their presence or absence in our lives and to absorb them into our thinking and being.

From here, Reverend John fleshes out his kingdom image with dizzying details, each worthy of careful consideration: the king of our kingdom of the soul is free will; his crown is charity; his garment is moral courage; his counsellors are knowledge and discernment, and they should live in a nearby palace called the rational faculty of the soul, and should be clad in moderation; the kingdom's judge is justice; the citizens are all the powers of the soul, which should be grounded in humility; and the Emperor over it all, of course, is the King of kings and Lord of lords.[8] Some of this is a repetition of the previously mentioned characteristics, only put together into

8. For all of this in context, see John of Ruusbroec, *Spiritual Espousals*, a452–752.

this image from Ruusbroec's medieval context. We could adapt the image to our modern society (the Mayor of Soul City is free will . . . the City Council is made up of knowledge and discernment, and they live in the Rational District, etc.); or we could draw the kingdom or create a chart—whatever will help us understand and absorb these virtues.

All of this is what it is to be at school in the kingdom of the soul. We can imagine dishevelled Reverend John standing before us in the classroom, directing our attention to the image of free will as a king who is crowned with charity and robed in moral courage and so on. The point is to learn these virtues so we might begin to live them. And it is Christ our Helper who guides and empowers our transformation. Reread those characteristics and the mind boggles at the depth and breadth of virtues all stacked together like stones and citizens forming a royal city. It is no wonder that one of the heirs of Ruusbroec's teaching, Thomas à Kempis, in one of the most popular books of all time, *The Imitation of Christ*, does not go much farther than this first leg of Reverend John's grand journey. We've already received a lifetime's worth of lessons on formative spirituality . . . and then some!

We need to pause and examine these foundational teachings. There is much to work with here in the kingdom of the soul. The ways Christ comes to us and the ways we go out to him in virtues are like seeds that need to be carefully sown into our lives and cultivated for fruitfulness. Like the Miyagi method of karate, the virtuous life requires dedication and repetition before it begins to become second nature. Most of it takes years, to be honest, and some surely takes a lifetime. This is nothing less than God's way becoming our way. But is there a more worthy investment of our efforts?

As we get into the next chapter, it is quite likely we'll find ourselves rushing back to this one. We must press on, but we'll soon see how important the lessons of the kingdom of the soul are for our quest.

Way-Stop #2: Reflection

Here we've been presented with the helper we've always wanted. But do we want him? What has our experience of Jesus Christ been to this point? For some, Jesus has been a welcome and dear part of our lives since childhood. Others met him at some point along the way, perhaps when he rescued them from desperate circumstances. Still others once knew him, became disillusioned with him, and moved on. Some, like Gandhi, say they are enamored of Jesus but put off by his followers. This disconnect is curious, since Jesus is consistently presented as keeping company with society's dregs, scalawags, castoffs, and flat-out sinners . . . people like us maybe. If we say we want Jesus but without the undesirables he insists on loving, maybe it isn't really Jesus we want. Nevertheless, perhaps encounters with some of Jesus's so-called followers have left us uninterested in becoming one of them. This really is understandable.

Whatever our experience of Jesus has been, we are invited here and now to encounter him anew. Difficult as it might be, it's probably a good idea for the journey we're on to set aside much, if not most, of what we think we know about this strange figure—even the good stuff—and try to make room for him to present himself as he really is. Much of what he said and did will likely challenge us, and some will make us uncomfortable and even rub us the wrong way. But if we stick with him we just may find a new fire being kindled.

To that end, every effort should be made to understand the life and ministry of Jesus of Nazareth. We do well to commit ourselves to knowing the Gospels, which might include the use of a good study Bible and maybe a commentary or two. Some might benefit from journaling through the Gospels, noting impressions, questions, struggles, and insights. We might practice *lectio divina* (divine reading), which can include: repeated readings of and meditation on short passages; engaging the imagination and senses to place ourselves in a biblical scene; noting what words or images stand out and what we think and feel and hear God saying to us; and responding with prayer and action.

Studying the Gospels is vital for bringing ourselves before Christ as our Teacher and Mentor, which is key to our schooling in the kingdom of the soul. Here, Christ comes to us and we go out to him in the dynamic shaping of our character through grace and gifts and virtues. Such lessons are essential for daily living in humility, charity, endurance, and justice. But they are also essential for our continued journey toward our true self in union with God, especially as our Helper begins to challenge us to follow him into the wilder and deeper adventure of life beyond our comfort zone.

Bearings

❖ *Location*: the Call > the Active Life > "the bridegroom comes; go out"

❖ *Key Concepts*: Christ as Helper; Christ's first coming (incarnation); Christ's second coming (daily presence); Christ's third coming (judgment); roots of virtue (humility, charity, patient endurance); the kingdom of the soul, with its characteristics and virtues and lessons

❖ *Practice*: studying the Gospels; *lectio divina*

3

CROSSING THE THRESHOLD

Gandalf stayed in the Shire for over two months. Then one evening, at
the end of June, soon after Frodo's plan had been finally arranged, he
suddenly announced that he was going off again next morning. "Only
for a short while, I hope," he said. . . . He spoke lightly, but it seemed to
Frodo that he looked rather worried.

—J. R. R. Tolkien, *The Fellowship of the Ring*

WE COULD STAY HERE forever, learning and training and studying and
lost in thought about the progress we're making. But it's time to
move on. We might not want to. That's why many people of faith never get
past the school of the kingdom of the soul. Of course we continue training
for the rest of our lives, developing those virtues like humility, justice, obedience, patient endurance, compassion, mercy, and the rest. But as we train
and learn and grow, we find that Christ our Helper is getting a bit elusive
and even inscrutable. His lessons grow more complicated, more challenging, and even a bit confusing. He seems to be leading us beyond the easy,
sunny, feel-good lessons we were becoming comfortable with. Did we ever
even know him at all?

Just as we feel we're getting a handle on things—getting a handle on
Christ—he seems to draw back. Like Obi-Wan telling Luke to let go and
use the Force, like Glinda telling Dorothy to follow the yellow brick road,
Jesus points the way but makes no assurances that he will be traveling with
us, at least not in an easily recognizable manner. He wants us to begin to
walk on our own sturdy legs—to walk by faith in him, yes, but to walk for

ourselves nonetheless. It's no wonder, then, that so many of our number decide they're content to stay in the easy realm of moralism of a rather superficial nature. To be sure, being schooled in the kingdom of the soul is vital, and the lessons to be learned and work to be done never end. But the point of it all is the meeting . . . and then everything that follows.

The First Meeting: God Alone and the Way of Unknowing

To meet him. The culmination of the first leg of the journey (the Call and the Active Life) is what Reverend John calls "meeting the Bridegroom," which is the culmination of our mystical earworm: "See, the bridegroom comes! Go out *to meet him!*" Of course we've already encountered him in the grace that enabled us to "See," in the reality-shifting revelation that "the bridegroom comes" as our Helper, and in our commitment to "go out" for his mentoring. But "to meet him" in a deeper and more transformative way is the goal of this part of the journey. As Ruusbroec explains, "In this meeting lies all our blessedness, as well as the beginning and end of all virtues; and without this meeting, no virtue is performed."[1]

All the previous descriptions of the virtuous life and the kingdom of the soul find their substance here. In fact, the concept of "meeting" the Bridegroom is the key to the entire journey. We are driven all along by the hope and faith that there might be meetings along the way, but that there will surely be a meeting—a marriage even—between sojourning seeker and divine Bridegroom in the end. What's more, only in the meeting will we find our true self.

The meeting with Christ our Bridegroom in this first stage has three parts. The first part is *being intent on God alone,* which is to say fixing the mind and will on God. This intention is driven by God's mystery, by the inability of humans to rightly name and comprehend God. This keeps us being drawn out and drawn in.

Many have spoken and written about the divine darkness and the inadequacy of attempts to name and describe God. It's one of the main points of the *via negativa,* the way of negation and of being purged of false notions about God that we and our culture and even our religion have constructed over time. Whatever we think we know and can name about God, God's God-ness immediately undoes and transcends. Whatever words or ideas we devise for describing God are insufficient, based not least on the very

---

1. John of Ruusbroec, *Spiritual Espousals,* a756.

fact that we limited beings have devised them. If we can think it, God can transcend it.

One of the most influential thinkers to explore this path was the man who wrote under the pseudonym Dionysius the Areopagite. He took his name from the member of the Areopagus in Athens converted under Paul's preaching (Acts 17:34), though he likely was a Syrian monk who lived in the late fifth to early sixth centuries. It seems unlikely that a faithful monk intended to actually fool people into thinking he was the biblical figure.[2] Some scholars posit that the choice of pseudonym was intentional for the purpose of invoking Paul's teaching, especially as the writer built his theology on Paul's reference in his Athens sermon to the "unknown God," which the Athenians "worship through [your] unknowing" (17:22–23).[3] Whatever the case, this so-called Pseudo-Dionysius, whose writing significantly influenced Ruusbroec and many others, offers some crucial insights for us at this juncture in our journey.

One of the most important concepts in Dionysian spirituality is the idea of "unknowing." Dionysius contrasts those committed to unknowing with "those caught up with the things of the world, who imagine that there is nothing beyond instances of individual being and who think that by their own intellectual resources they can have a direct knowledge of him who has made the shadows his hiding place."[4] Basically, we can try to figure God out through our own ego trips and intellectualizing, or we can let go and get to know God up close and personal on God's own terms. If we desire "initiation into the divine"—described as the "transcendent Cause of all things"—then "we should posit and ascribe to [the Cause] all the affirmations we make in regard to beings, and, more appropriately, we should negate all

---

2. Nevertheless, his reputation as the actual Pauline convert gave his writings considerable authority in many circles, and the translation of his works into Latin around the ninth century resulted in his mystical theology exercising significant influence in the West through the Middle Ages. It wasn't until the early days of the Reformation era that Erasmus voiced doubts about the author's identity. But by then, the unknown figure had imprinted his theology into the thinking of many of the greatest medieval theologians, from Bonaventure and Thomas Aquinas, to Meister Eckhart and John of Ruusbroec and John of the Cross, and on to today's renewed interest in his Neoplatonic Christian theology.

3. Stang, "Dionysius, Paul." Stang suggests "worship through [your] unknowing" as a legitimate alternative to the traditional translation, "worship as unknown."

4. Pseudo-Dionysius, *Mystical Theology*, 136.

these affirmations, since [the Cause] surpasses all being."[5] With this, Dionysius lays out his project for union with God by way of unknowing.

Clearly we need to break this down a bit. This type of spirituality is possibly unfamiliar and likely strange to most in the Christian West with its focus on the attributes of God (e.g., all-powerful, all-knowing, etc.). For Dionysius, unknowing means even the divine light must be left behind in exchange for divine darkness. And this is accomplished through the process of negation, known in Greek as *apophatic* (literally, saying no) theology, and in the Latin tradition as the *via negativa*.[6] However, in order to reach the way of negation, it can be helpful to first follow the *cataphatic* (affirming) way. Dionysius says that the visible, known things of God are the starting place for unknowing. God reveals himself through symbols and imagery suitable to our human nature in order to lead us to the higher, mystical path of Godlikeness. We first say all that we can about God in the form of divine attributes, images, forms, figures, and the like. But eventually we find this way failing—our language falters until only silence remains in the realm of God's indescribability.

At that point we must turn to the apophatic way. Dionysius uses the image of sculptors carving statues: "They remove every obstacle to the pure view of the hidden image, and simply by this act of clearing aside they show up the beauty which is hidden."[7] So, we can think of this process as "clearing aside" everything in our conception of God that ultimately falls short. With this, Dionysius begins a relentless process of saying what God, the Cause of all, is *not*—not a material body, not perceptible, not soul or mind, not number or order, not power, not kingship, not light, not life, not eternity or time, not wisdom, neither one nor oneness, not sonship or fatherhood, "nothing known to us or to any other being."[8] And finally, in a bit of a humorous "meta" statement, Dionysius concludes by saying that God "is beyond assertion and denial," which is to say, beyond the process of unknowing and apophatic theology.

For Dionysius true transformation comes from the inside out, from inner union with the radically transcendent Cause of all being. Such

5. Pseudo-Dionysius, *Mystical Theology*, 136.

6. Sarah Coakley stresses a distinction between the two, noting that "the Greek noun *apophasis* can also convey the meaning of 'revelation' . . . thus giving it richer overtones than the Latin." Coakley, "Introduction," 9n30.

7. Pseudo-Dionysius, *Mystical Theology*, 138.

8. Pseudo-Dionysius, *Mystical Theology*, 140–41.

transformation can be experienced only by unknowing, by letting go of all we think we know or ever could know about God, as well as about ourselves.[9] Only then can we begin to behold God as God really is and ourselves as we really are, and to experience increasingly intimate and transformational union.

Heavily influenced by the Dionysian tradition, Ruusbroec presents the same process in describing our meeting with Christ the Bridegroom, the first aspect of which is being intent and focused on God alone. It is because of God's sublime unknowability, says Reverend John, that we first need to look at God in whatever light we have and come to know God by whatever names have proven faithful and true. This is essential for keeping the mind and will focused on God. God's unknowability is conceptually true, but for the practical purposes of our formative journey, we first need to embrace all we can rightly affirm about God. We should resist trite platitudes, of course, and erase distorting caricatures. But the God revealed positively in Scripture, and especially in the Gospels, is a helpful lantern for approaching the dark *via negativa*.

Intertwined with this first part of the meeting is the second part—*not intending or loving anything as much as, or more than, God*. While Reverend John mentioned "intent" in the first aspect of the meeting, now he adds "loving," so it is not simply a mental fixation but always a willed and active devotion toward God. He also describes the connection of this God-focused desire in terms of four loves: the love within God, which is the divine Person of the Holy Spirit; the love within us, which is God's grace and our good will; the love between us and God, which is holy desire rising up to God's glory; and the outflowing love between us and our neighbors.[10]

These four loves are really the fourfold response to divine love—as 1 John 4:19 says, "We love because God first loved us," which John Wesley called "the sum of all religion, the genuine model of Christianity."[11] Within this fourfold love, then, are the characteristics of God-focused desire. The result is self-mastery, bringing our often far-flung and confusing desires and intentions into focus on God alone, and all as a response to God's loving inclination toward us. We think of the prayer of the great mystic Julian

9. Stang refers to "apophatic anthropology," saying that the self must also become "unsaid" or "cleared away" in the process of uniting with the "unknown God." Stang, "Dionysius, Paul," 16–18.

10. See John of Ruusbroec, *Mirror of Eternal Blessedness*, ll. 100–130.

11. Wesley, *Explanatory Notes*, 1 John 4:19.

of Norwich (1342–ca. 1423), whose writings are the earliest surviving English language works by a woman: "God, of your goodness give me yourself, for you are enough for me . . . only in you do I have everything."[12] Her words are all the more touching when we consider that she prayed them in the midst of an illness (possibly the result of intense mystical devotion) so severe it was believed she might die.

The other side of the coin of being intent on God alone is this denial of any other intention, for to be intent on God alone necessarily means being intent on nothing else. Reverend John claims that this dual posture of loving intention towards God and rejection of all else results in an assurance of eternal blessedness and forgiveness of sins. The haranguing inner monologue of "Is this okay?" and "Am I okay?" is silenced in the singular focus on God's affirming love. We take to heart Julian of Norwich's vision of Jesus speaking to her in the midst of her painful purgation: "He comforts readily and sweetly with his words, and says: But all will be well, and every kind of thing will be well."[13]

All will be well. Such assurance strengthens our faith and drives us toward a more vibrant and virtuous life both inwardly and outwardly. Both of these—a God-focused mind and will, and the refusal of competing foci— are the first two aspects of meeting Christ, which is to say coming to know the eternal Christ as more than simply a good moral teacher.

Crossing the Threshold: Knowing We Can't Know

The third part of the deeper meeting with Christ our Helper and Bridegroom serves as both the ending of the first stage, the Active Life, and the transition to the next stage. This third part of the meeting is *to enthusiastically and passionately rest in God*, above all others and even above all God's gifts and our virtuous works. This resting is different from the more active seeking and practicing of virtues, which have so far characterized the first stage of the journey. In fact, the resting is the reason for such seeking and practicing. It is, after all, Christ the Bridegroom whom we are after, not the virtues or even the virtuous life themselves.

Our efforts to "See" the ways in which "the bridegroom comes," and to "go out" to him as devoted apprentices, were all done in order "to meet him," which now includes resting in him. We might imagine ourselves at

12. Julian of Norwich, *Showings* (Long Text), 1.6.
13. Julian of Norwich, *Showings* (Short Text), xiii.

this point running through a crowd of people, all clamoring for our attention and affections, and falling into Christ's arms. Resting in the Beloved above all else fulfills the Active Life, causing Reverend John to refer to the completed stage as "perfection" (of this first part).

This point of transition is an example of what Joseph Campbell calls Crossing the First Threshold, explaining that "the crossing of the threshold is the first step into the sacred zone of the universal source. . . . The adventure is always and everywhere a passage beyond the veil of the known into the unknown."[14] Reverend John commends those who have come this far on the journey, explaining that this first, Active Life stage is necessary for anyone who wants to be considered a disciple of Jesus Christ. But he also begins to tease us with the promise of much more: "The person who thus lives in this perfection . . . will frequently be touched in his desire to see, to know, to understand who this Bridegroom, Christ, is."[15]

Such understanding leading to union is the point of the whole journey, yet the more we understand, the more we want to know. Our understanding begins to break down. We've begun to get to know Christ through our study and our devotion; but do we really *know* him? As he says to his befuddled disciples at one point, "What if you were to see the Son of Man ascend to where he was before?" (John 6:62). He seems to be saying, "If you think this teaching is hard, wait'll you get a load of the Trinity!" For some, their patience with Jesus's challenging lessons and leadership has reached its limit, with the result that "many of his disciples turned back and no longer followed him" (John 6:66). So, how will it go for us?

Now, like a kung fu master employing Zen riddles to challenge and grow his student, Reverend John offers this startling conclusion to the first stage of the journey: the highest knowledge we can have about God in the Active Life is that God is unknowable. All we can know is that we can't know. All we can comprehend is that we can't comprehend. We did our best to piece together a sketch of God, but in the end we must admit that it is destined to fall infinitely short of the real thing.

The Dark Night Rises

We have reached our limit. If we wish to continue, we must let go. It's an unsettling realization. This is the real meaning of "the dark night of the

14. Campbell, *Hero with Thousand Faces*, 67.
15. John of Ruusbroec, *Spiritual Espousals*, a826–29.

soul." The expression has entered popular culture to simply mean a difficult time, possibly resulting in doubt and self-examination. But the person responsible for the expression, John of the Cross (1542–91), was of the same school of spirituality as John of Ruusbroec and was likely influenced by his work. So, his famous expression signifies much more than "a rough patch," though difficult circumstances might be part of our challenge to let go.

John of the Cross was a mystic, poet, spiritual director, and creative theologian who, having run afoul of the religious authorities of his day, spent nine months being flogged and starved in a lice-infested prison cell. But while his little body wasted away nearly to the point of death, his soul was meeting God in a way only possible through complete abandonment. He composed poems in his mind about the way of divine darkness leading to divine light. Finally, after a daring escape from prison, John was able to make his way to safety and recovery. He went on to record and expound upon the poetry that had sustained him—about the God who had sustained him—through his desperate trials.

So, more than just shorthand for a tough time, the true "dark night" includes the deep struggle of unknowing and utterly abandoning ourselves to God.[16] As is likely becoming clearer, the "dark night" is a much broader and deeper concept than our cultural catchall has come to denote. In fact, John of the Cross leads us through multiple planes of the "dark night," which consist of "nights" on the level of the senses (body) and of the spirit (mind), both actively pursued by seeking and passively experienced by abandoning oneself to the work of God alone. It's very similar to what we are beginning to see in the teaching of John of the Cross's forerunner, John of Ruusbroec, and it is very challenging but very necessary if we are to share life fully with God.

The especially good news in all this is that this is what it is to see God spiritually. We are beginning to awaken to a new way of knowing, by way of unknowing. At this point, Reverend John turns to the story of Jesus and Zacchaeus, the short-statured tax collector who climbed a tree so he could see over the crowd and catch a glimpse of Jesus (Luke 19:1–10). Zacchaeus's desire to see and its fulfilment in actually connecting him with Jesus are like the "meeting" in this first stage. What comes next, however, is what separates the potential heroes from the faint of heart, those who press on from those who turn back and no longer follow him. Jesus tells the socially despised little man, "Zacchaeus, come down immediately. I must stay at

---

16. See John of the Cross, *Ascent of Mount Carmel* and *Dark Night*.

your house today" (5). This is Christ our Teacher's challenge to us to cross the threshold of the known and follow him into the unknown of the next stage of the journey. But in order to answer the challenge and cross that threshold, we must face its guardian.

Reason: The Guardian at the Gate

In most hero stories, the threshold guardian is a monster of some kind, although, like the irresistible song of the Sirens in *The Odyssey*, it can be deceptively appealing. For Ruusbroec's journey, the threshold guardian takes the form of Reason. The struggle here is to get out of our own way. However, like the Sirens' song, Reason is entrancing. We encounter this guardian in our demand for answers, in our appeals to intellect and our reliance on understanding to figure everything out, often before we will take one more step. Most of us are not only content to stay in the realm controlled by Reason, we are even proud of our unwillingness to cross the line into the unknowable and seemingly unreasonable. Far from being any sort of tyrant or monster, Reason is our champion!

Continuing with the image of little Zacchaeus descending the tree to accompany Jesus, Reverend John explains, "This hasty descent is nothing other than a flowing-down with longing and with love into the abyss of the Godhead, which no understanding can reach in created light [as opposed to uncreated, divine light]. But where intellect remains outside, there longing and love go in."[17] This image of a threshold—an outside and an inside designating two different realms—holds a key concept for the journey: intellect can't come in, but longing and love are welcome. It is Reason that blocks the way to the deeper parts of ourselves and our journey with God.

Reason stands at the doorway to the inner journey and says, "You don't want to go in there. You have things mostly figured out. You have God mostly figured out. If you keep going, the life you've built will probably fall apart. Also, and I hate to bring this up, but there are parts of yourself that you'll find in there that are better left alone. Who knows what God will do with you if you follow him into the unknown and let him get his hands on those hidden things. You're much better off staying out here and working things out for yourself. There are plenty of books and media and people with all kinds of answers out here. You've got this!"

17. John of Ruusbroec, *Spiritual Espousals*, a853–55.

This view of Reason as something to be overcome might seem counterintuitive to us (which actually proves the point). Aren't we really after *greater* understanding, not less? The answer is yes and no. We are after greater understanding, but it is not *our* understanding that we're after. Instead, we should recall that the third part of our deeper meeting with Christ is to rest in God alone. And God is incomprehensible, beyond even the greatest understanding we can attain. What we are after here is a deepening faith in *God's* understanding. Reason opposes the way of unknowing that is necessary to true Godlikeness in our understanding and being. Our need for control can only threaten the journey. What's really happening is that our false self is blocking the way to our true self.

In the Belly of the Beast

The confrontation with Reason as threshold guardian is dangerous because it threatens the stability of our world as we have known it, a world controlled by ego. And if our journey and its God have their way with us, then we will likely no longer fit in with that world's order when we emerge. There will be a breakdown of our self-reliance and even our self-understanding. We've spent years constructing a life around our false self and its illusions of control, around a dualistic worldview that easily sorts things into black or white, good or bad, this or that. But in order to move toward the divine Other, in which our own otherness is also found, the well-ordered answers of intellect must be overcome.

While there is a place down the road for the ascent of intellect, the descent of desire is now essential for moving past this threshold, which gives way to the inner journey. Reason wants to go higher, building more floors onto the skyscraper in order to get a wider view and more details and answers. But the lofty perspective of intellect, at this point, is the very thing that stands in the way of the next stage. Love, on the other hand, longs to go deeper, to follow the Beloved even into the dark underworld if that's what it takes to be together. So, the question here is, Do we really trust God? Do we want God enough to let go of ourselves?

This letting go is like a death to self, which is essential if the journey is to continue. Our ego, with its need to control and dominate and protect us from appearing weak and insignificant, has no place here. Ego will team up with Reason and fight to hold on to power, even relying on potentially good things like religion and self-help to keep us in line. But the rest of the journey lies outside the boundary lines. We can't go on without going in, going down, denying ourselves and taking up our cross.

After running from God and from his prophetic calling, Jonah winds up in the sea where he is consumed by a great fish. Inside the fish for three days and nights, Jonah encounters God. He repents of his running and finally lets go of control, declaring, "From deep in the realm of the dead I called for help, and you listened to my cry" (Jonah 2:2). Similarly, wayward Pinocchio is separated from his creator and father, Geppetto. He finally reconnects with him inside the dark belly of a dogfish or whale. And so for us, our journey can continue only if we let go and trust the incomprehensible God and allow ourselves to be swallowed in the darkness of the divine embrace.

Our character has been formed in the school of the kingdom of the soul, increasingly shaping us into more of a heavenly creature and less of a worldly and selfish one. As John of the Cross puts it, "That night of purifying contemplation lulled to sleep and deadened all the inordinate movements of the passions and appetites in the house of sense."[18] We have set our mind and heart more and more on God and less and less on "the house of sense," which is to say ego and material concerns. To be clear, unknowing and resting in God are not goals to be accomplished or mastered before we continue. Like Dorothy emerging into the Technicolor world of Oz and Neo surveying the schematic illusion of the Matrix, this is merely a transition to a new beginning in a new reality. Unknowing and resting are ways of interacting with God more and more on God's terms, and we will find them to be necessary and useful postures as our journey continues.

We see all of this perfectly exemplified in Jesus. From being plunged into the baptismal waters and then immediately driven into the trials of the wilderness, to his suffering and crucifixion and entombment in death, Jesus was no stranger to the belly of the beast. But in the face of such circumstances he fully fixed his focus and abandoned his being to the powerful, loving embrace of the Father and the Spirit. To those asking him for a sign, Jesus declared, "None will be given except the sign of the prophet Jonah. For as Jonah was three days and three nights in the belly of a huge fish, so the Son of Man will be three days and three nights in the heart of the earth" (Matt 12:39–40). The way of Jesus inevitably leads past signs and answers and into the embrace of darkness.

18. John of the Cross, *Dark Night*, 1.2.

Now Jesus says to us what he said to Zacchaeus: "Come down so I can dwell in your house." Our "house" in this case is the essence of our being in what Reverend John calls the "abyss of the Godhead," the eternally deep darkness that we've tried so hard to avoid. What lies ahead? We don't know, can't know, and that's the point. The treasure we seek—God and our true self—lies in the unknowing. This is not the time for maps. We must walk the road as it opens before us and learn to, as someone said, let it be.

Way-Stop #3: Reflection

Things might be getting confusing, perhaps frustrating, or even a bit scary. We probably read books like this one seeking answers: "The Three Keys to a Perfect Life" or "God and the True Self in Five E-Z Steps." We've come seeking illumination and yet here we are in the dark night, learning to unlearn, coming to know that we can't know. Instead of finding ourselves, we're being challenged to lose ourselves. And what of that business about how we can't really know God? Isn't that the opposite of what it means to be saved and a lot of what Jesus said?

Such issues will be addressed as we continue. But it's important to be honest about these fears and frustrations. Concepts like the unknowability and darkness of God are likely strange to modern Christians, especially in the Western tradition, and such thinking might even seem un-Christian to some. On the other hand, some will feel justified in their belief that there really are no answers, that people of faith are grasping at straws and so we should just cobble together whatever belief system suits us. Still others might simply be impatient to get on with it. The truth is, all of these reactions helpfully reveal our reliance on ego and Reason, our resistance to letting go of control and opening up to the unknown. Our need for answers and clear directions is subtle but ever present. Even our difficulty in admitting this about ourselves only proves the point.

We might do what we can to embrace this letting go through the practices of solitude and silence, including both planned and spontaneous times spent alone and in quiet. Such times might be found in the moments before getting out of bed, a morning or noon or evening quiet time, driving with the radio off, periods without TV and social media, and so on. Silence can even include holding our tongue, keeping our opinions to ourselves sometimes. In solitude and silence we practice letting go of distractions and words and information and control as we also practice listening and simply being. As thoughts arise we simply acknowledge them and practice letting them go. A repeated mantra or sacred word ("Jesus," "Yahweh," "Abba," "Spirit," etc.) or a memorized Scripture verse can help calm and focus our thinking. While the discipline might require some reason and control in order to practice it, it is preparing us for the much deeper solitude and silence of regularly resting in the unknowable and unfathomable God.

So here we are. Here we must simply be. We don't have to pretend to have answers anymore. Perhaps we can begin to recognize some implications for our everyday lives and the many things that are out of our control. It's freeing, really . . . frightening and freeing. But we can take comfort in the fact that Christ our Helper and Teacher has led us here. He has been here before us, and he is here with us, though he might seem distant and even altogether absent. However, at this point we must quiet the inner monologue, stop thinking with our eyes, and let the journey take us where it will take us.

Follow the yellow brick road.

Bearings

- *Location*: the Call > the Active Life > "to meet him"

- *Key Concepts*: meeting; apophatic theology; *via negativa*; cataphatic theology; unknowability of God; unknowing; purgation; dark night; threshold crossing; Reason as guardian; belly of the beast; abyss of the Godhead

- *Practice*: solitude and silence

Part II

THE ROAD

4

The Making of a Hero

*"Well, here's where we all find out if we was meant to be cowboys,"
Augustus said—for he had no doubt that Deets would soon be proved
right about the coming storm.*

—Larry McMurtry, Lonesome Dove

*W*HO AM I? It's not just a question; it very well might be *the* question.
And we don't ask it just once. It's a question that comes up again and
again—in adolescence, in early adulthood, in marriage and parenthood,
in middle age, in retirement, in old age. Just when we think we have it, the
answer slips away. We thought we were one thing, but then we realize or
decide we're another. Is there anything true about us, anything fundamentally real that might serve as a foundation to build on, an identity to live
into? In hero stories much of this question is answered on the Road, which
is the part of the journey we're now approaching. Vladimir Propp calls this
long section Guidance to the Object of Search, while Joseph Campbell calls
it Initiation and the Road of Trials.[1] There is sublime joy along the way,
but there are also considerable trials that must be faced. On the Road we
encounter struggles that reveal the nature of our quest and of ourselves.
It might bring out our worst, and it might even drive us to abandon the
whole journey. Many do. But, for those who press on, the Road is the place
of transformation and the path to the treasure we seek, as well as many
treasures we never knew to seek.

1. Propp, *Morphology of the Folktale*, 50–51; Campbell, *Hero with Thousand Faces*,
81–90.

Who am I? The question is inseparably intertwined with the desire for more to life. There must be more to life, and there must be more to *me*. Like Cinderella, the mistreated stepdaughter and servant girl destined to become a benevolent princess. Like Aladdin, the poor street urchin who gains the love of a princess and eventually inherits a kingdom. Such characters (and there are many) have two primary things in common: 1) they are diamonds in the rough who, despite appearances and circumstances, have nobility and heroism within them; and 2) they have the aid of helpers, as well as a meaningful totem or magical agent of some kind (glass slipper, lamp). But the key is that the helpers and enchanted objects serve only to reveal the heroism that already lives inside the main character.

So the answer is yes, there is something fundamental about our being that is not only real but is deeply connected to the essence of reality itself. Shockingly, this reality is true of every human being, though almost every person on earth is unaware of it. But there is also an identity to live into, a supernatural gift that can turn the lowliest and roughest of us into the noble hero we're meant to be. This gift is not readily present in every human, though it is available to everyone. Instead, it is a transformative blessing that has to be received in order to do its work. Indeed, it *must* be received and allowed to do its work if our journey is to continue. We will soon hit the Road for the second leg of our adventure—but first, the making of a hero.

Magic Mirror

In the Snow White stories, the evil queen employs a magic mirror to reveal the truth about her beauty and her status as fairest in the land. When Snow White comes of age, however, the mirror reveals the truth that the young maiden has surpassed the queen in beauty. Overcome with jealousy, the wicked queen plots to destroy her competition. While there are plenty of insights into human nature in Snow White, there's something about the magic mirror that is especially appropriate for us. First, there is indeed a magic mirror in our story. And second, *we* are the magic mirror.

There is a long tradition of likening the human soul to a mirror—from Paul's teaching that we now see "through a mirror" (1 Cor 13:12) and that we "with unveiled faces see the Lord's glory as though reflected in a mirror" (2 Cor 3:18); to Augustine of Hippo (354–430) explaining that "what we have been trying to do is somehow to see him by whom we were made by means of this image which we ourselves are, as through a mirror";[2] and on to our humble guide, John of Ruusbroec.

In his book *A Mirror of Eternal Blessedness* (written in his beloved forest community), Reverend John writes that every human has God's image impressed upon his or her soul, so that our created life is one with God's image and one with our life that is safely secured with God in eternity.[3] This is true of each human, so that "we are all one, united in our eternal image, that is God's image and the origin of us all—of our life and our becoming."[4] The fundamental truth of our being is that we are all one in God's image (which Ruusbroec explains is God the Son), regardless of our differences and the many ways we devise to divide ourselves. Imagine how the world might be if we would recognize in each other that divine beauty and eternal value!

So we don't miss the profound revelation here, we need to state this clearly before going on to break it down: the essence of who we are as humans is ceaseless relationship with God. At the core of our being, we are bound to God, and our essence as humans is not a substance but a relationship—a relationship of union with God. This is the *potential* prince or princess in each of us, heroic sons and daughters of the King and diamonds in the rough.

This Is Us

Reverend John calls this state of every human in relationship with God "natural unity," and it is experienced in three parts. The first part of this natural state of unity is what we've just mentioned, which he calls *essential unity*. It says we are united with God both within ourselves and above ourselves in the essence of our being in God. We can think of our aliveness as money, which is held in a heavenly safe but is also accessible via a card that we carry on us, which is our soul. And the account is a joint account, held by both God and us. It's a crude metaphor, but we need to begin to get a handle on these concepts of *essence* and *essential unity* before moving on. This essential unity is responsible for our being, says Ruusbroec,

---

2. Augustine of Hippo, *Trin.* 15.3.14.

3. See John of Ruusbroec, *Mirror of Eternal Blessedness*, 1672–75.

4. John of Ruusbroec, *Mirror of Eternal Blessedness*, l. 861.

and without it "we would fall into nothingness and be annihilated."[5] (Now there's a pleasant thought we can share at parties.)

So, in addition to the vital revelation that our very essence is relationship to God, another revelation here is the divine origin of our lives—both our larger existence and our daily aliveness. In his first book (the bootlegged one), *The Realm of Lovers*, Reverend John describes our essential unity beautifully and powerfully: "[This essence of the soul] hangs in God, is immobile, and is higher than the uppermost heaven and deeper than the bottom of the sea, and broader than all the world with all the elements, for spiritual nature transcends all corporeal nature."[6] This essential level is the natural realm of God in which God alone works, for God is the "essence of essences, the life of lives, and the beginning and sustenance of all creatures."[7] The origin stories of many heroic characters include divine and/ or royal parentage. We are no different, and in many ways this journey we're on is about realizing and owning and living our true identity as children of God and heirs of God's kingdom here and now and forever. But remember that this includes everyone.

The second aspect of the natural unity between all humans and God is *unity of the spirit* (or *mind*). It is basically the same as essential unity but is like its flip side, because unity of the spirit is active where essential unity is passive. Essential unity is concerned with our being, while unity of the spirit concerns our thinking and emotions. By equating the spirit with the mind, however, we are not speaking merely of brain functions. Our brain is involved, as we are embodied beings, but it is all informing and shaping our life that continues even after our body gives out (though we should also understand that our ultimate destiny is resurrection and everlasting life as embodied beings).

To dive a bit deeper into the waters of theological anthropology (that is, the nature of humanity as associated with God), what we're dealing with here are the classic "higher faculties" of the human mind: memory, intellect, and will. Memory here is akin to mindfulness or self-reflection. Intellect is our reason and our capacity for understanding. And our will is what drives us, our choices and goals and actions. These are key components that make us human. Whereas in the essential unity these faculties are grounded in God's essence (God's "God-ness") and thus are beyond our control, here in

---

5. John of Ruusbroec, *Spiritual Espousals*, b38.

6. John of Ruusbroec, *Realm of Lovers*, ll. 272–75.

7. John of Ruusbroec, *Realm of Lovers*, ll. 277–78.

the unity of the spirit they are also grounded in our spirit or mind, in which case we have the capacity to exercise and develop those same faculties. In this way they become tools for answering our present question: *Who am I?*

The third component of our natural unity is *unity of the heart.* This is the lowest and outermost aspect of the natural union of all humans with God. It is the natural origin of our bodily activity and our senses, our appetites and desires. It is something like our basic, animal "life force" that animates us and keeps our body living. Still, even on our basest and most fundamental level, each human is united with God.

It might be helpful to see how this connects with Jesus's Great Commandment: "Love the Lord your God with all your heart and with all your soul and with all your mind and with all your strength" (Mark 12:30; see Deut 6:5). (Note: We do well to understand that this is as much a promise as a commandment, as if Jesus is saying "*You will be able to* love the Lord your God with all your being." Which, in a nutshell, is what this whole quest is about.) For our purposes we can understand what Jesus calls our "strength" to be primarily our bodily and material life, and our "heart" to be our drive and desires, and both are mostly encompassed in Ruusbroec's "unity of the heart."[8] What Jesus calls our "mind" entails our thoughts and feelings, seen in Ruusbroec's "unity of the spirit." And our "soul" can be understood as our aliveness that binds all the others—all of our being—together, akin to Ruusbroec's "essential unity." All of which is the natural unity between humans and God.

So, what Jesus and Reverend John are presenting in their own respective ways is a picture of our whole being, which has the potential to be employed in total participation in the life and love of God.[9] This is an initial glimpse of our true self. Therefore, says Reverend John, when we look into the magic mirror that is our very being—both in what we see and what we can't see—each of us is the product and manifestation of a relationship with the God of the universe. Not too shabby!

8. In the Bible, including Jesus's usage, the word for "heart" connotes the idea of the center of our being, seen in our will, drive, and desires. So for Ruusbroec's schema, this would straddle or overlap his "unity of the heart" and "unity of the spirit."

9. For another survey of the process of coming to love God with our whole being, see Willard, *Renovation of the Heart.* I also explore this in Pelfrey, *Still Moving.*

Christ the Helper's "Bibbidi-Bobbidi-Boo"

What is happening at this point on the journey is something of a pause for self-assessment, a breather in which our guide is explaining to us the person we are and the person we're becoming. As we mentioned, our natural unity reveals the *potential* each of us has to become the hero who waits within us. As with Cinderella and Aladdin and others, our true nobility and heroism require the aid of a magical agent if we are going to fully become who we're made to be. We are diamonds in the rough, and we need our Helper to do the transforming work in our lives to make all our facets shine.

But here's the surprise: Christ's "bibbidi-bobbidi-boo" (to borrow some magic words from Fairy Godmother) has already begun transforming our being. It started when we accepted the invitation to this journey. It's what Jesus called being "born again from above" (John 3:3) and Paul called becoming a "new creation in Christ" (2 Cor 5:17). Ruusbroec wants to pause and make sure we realize what's happening. The way he puts it is that our *natural* unity with God must be *supernaturally* adorned (i.e., made over). It's an interesting image that really does hearken to the classic tales, with Fairy Godmother magically transforming Cinderella into the belle of the ball, or Genie magically transforming Aladdin into the fabulous Prince Ali. Likewise (though infinitely more amazing), Christ our Helper transforms the natural unity each of us has with God just by being human into a supernatural union that is unique to those who have answered the Call and undertaken the first leg of the journey, the Active Life.

All of the time we've spent learning from Christ our Helper and Teacher in the school of the kingdom of the soul, he has been transforming our natural unity with God into supernatural union. The unity of the heart (our strength and bodily desires) is being transformed by conforming to the model of Christ. The unity of the spirit (our mind and higher faculties) is being transformed by God's grace empowering us to live the virtuous life, seen especially in a life marked by the "theological virtues" of faith, hope, and love. The essential unity (the highest one, our essence and soul) does not necessarily need to be supernaturally adorned, since it is grounded in God. However, our experience of it is becoming more tangible as we've fixed our minds and hearts on God and are coming to trust and rest in God above all else.

All of this is the active fulfillment of Jesus's Great Commandment/ Promise, that we will be empowered to love God with our whole being. As we've been going out to meet Christ for training, he's been coming to us with the gift of supernatural adornment, transforming us from poor beggars into heroic daughters and sons of the King. We're on our way to fully and completely loving God and our neighbors, including all people, animals, and the natural world. To "love" is to selflessly and even sacrificially will and work for the good of the other, and surely there is nothing more heroic than that!

This is all the result of God's grace and God's essence working in us, though it requires our ongoing participation through virtues and disciplines. At this point, one more thing should be understood about the nature of our journey: Ruusbroec's path builds on itself, so that one stage is not left behind for the next. The lessons and work of the Active Life (the light of grace, exploring the Gospels, practicing virtues and cultivating character, focusing on and resting in God, etc.) only continue and grow from here.

How to See Ourselves

See. Before moving on we should note that Ruusbroec's motif, our mystical earworm, has started again: "See, the bridegroom comes! Go out to meet him!" We went through its stages in the first leg of our journey, the Active Life. Now we are beginning the next stage, which Ruusbroec calls the Inner Life. The good news is we're already addressing what it is that Reverend John wants us to "See," namely the people we are. The *what* of seeing is that, as humans, we are essentially a relationship with God and a mirror through which God is imaged and reflected—to ourselves, to the world, and back to God. This is our natural unity. Furthermore, what we should see is that, as reborn and committed apprentices of Jesus Christ, our natural unity is supernaturally adorned with the capacity for transformation into more fully realized humans who live in perfect loving union with God (and so, with each other and all creation). We are currently on the journey toward that kind of union, in which we find our true selves.

Now Reverend John explains the *how* of seeing. Here he recalls our present state of resting in the dark embrace of the Godhead. We are emerging from the belly of the beast into a shadowy borderland between stages. And, while we might have come to understand some important things about ourselves, we are also beginning to walk the way of unknowing, of letting go of much of what we've come to believe about God and ourselves. So, our ability to truly see ourselves is somewhat hazy. Therefore, in order to undertake the arduous coming journey through the Inner Life, we need three things to see more clearly and to begin to know ourselves. (We might be starting to notice that Reverend John likes to break his concepts down into parts, often three.)

The first thing necessary to "See" our true selves is *the light of God's grace* experienced in a higher way than at the beginning of the Active Life (remember our earlier section on "Divine Sight" and prevenient and meritorious grace). This inner illumination of God's grace is like a candle in a lantern or glass vessel, because it warms and illuminates us within and shines from within us outward. In other words, our continued cooperation with and trust in God's work helps us to see the truth about the world inside us and the world outside us, that there is more to life and more to us.

The second thing needed for this illumination, which comes from the first, is *detachment*, what Reverend John calls "a stripping away of alien images and of busyness of heart, so that, with respect to all created things, we can be free, unassailed by images, detached, and empty."[10] Such detachment and emptiness are far from being aloof and blank. They are, in fact, the opposite—the ability to be present and aware. It can be as simple as putting the minor distractions around us in their place, and as complex as overcoming the ghosts and demons that plague us inside and out. That's why it can come only from cooperation with God's grace enabling us to see things as they really are.

Building on this detachment, the third thing necessary to "See" in the Inner Life is *freedom*, which is to say the ability to turn within ourselves without being hindered and overwhelmed by distracting thoughts and images. Some ghosts might linger, but now they drift in and out without any real power in our lives. We are beginning to be freed from bondage to our false self and misguided ideas about reality. The aim is to be able to see clearly so we can make the inner journey and live into our supernaturally adorned union with God.

All of this might shed new light on Jesus's statements like "I am in the Father and the Father is in me" (John 14:11), and "I came from the Father and entered the world; now I am leaving the world and going back to the Father" (16:28). Jesus had a deep faith and confidence that stemmed from this essential reality we are now discovering. This is not to discount the extra nuance his unique identity as the Second Person of the Trinity brings to such statements. But still, we have much to learn about our fundamental nature from looking at the illumination, detachment, and freedom

10. John of Ruusbroec, *Spiritual Espousals*, b24–26.

exemplified in Jesus and his understanding of his life as essentially ground-ed in God. His life originated with the Father, housed the Father and was housed by the Father, and was destined to return to the eternal embrace of the Father. This is our reality as well.

Way-Stop #4: Reflection

The ideas in this chapter might be a bit challenging, but hopefully they're encouraging as well. Some things we're encountering might be difficult for us to accept, not just on an intellectual or theological level, but on a personal level. We've mentioned distractions and ghosts and demons—the events and memories and thoughts and fears that hinder us; and depending on their number and their nature, self-acceptance might be difficult. This might be especially challenging given the extraordinary "self" we are begin-ning to discover. With all that distracts us and haunts us and harangues us, what evidence is there that we are fundamentally united with God? If this is our thinking, perhaps sticking with the journey will begin to open us a bit more to this reality. Looking more closely at how we are being supernatu-rally transformed might help us to accept this truth about our relationship with God and, thus, move closer to our true selves.

On the other hand, maybe this is all an eye-opening relief. Maybe, despite our past or our shortcomings or our struggles, there's something about us that makes us hero material after all. And so, maybe we can accept this as the amazing news it is and continue on the journey of transforma-tion. With this in mind, we might benefit from a brief assessment of things, to get our bearings and maybe to grapple with a few of the concepts before we build on them.

The light of God's grace shines within us and through us, revealing distracting images of one kind or another so they can be removed, and thus enabling us as illumined sojourners to move freely onward, which is to say inward. We are gaining some facility with the practices and training of the Active Life, and we have crossed the First Threshold and passed its guard-ian, Reason, at least beginning to learn to let go of the need for control as we learn to trust and rest in God. We have learned some things about our true nature as essentially united with God, that we as humans are fundamentally a relationship even more than a substance. And we have begun to catch a glimpse of the person we're becoming on the journey, that the natural unity of our body, mind, and soul with God is being supernaturally transformed and perfected.

In light of these revelations, we might take on the practice of celebration. This can include singing and dancing and laughing, enjoying performances and creative arts and perhaps creating our own art or crafts. We can fully participate in holidays and celebratory events, even turning an ordinary day or weekend into a festival of joy with the food and drink and activities and people we love. We can include anything that reminds us that we and those around us are expressions of God—the most joyous being in the universe—and that we all are one.

This practice is all the more important as we will be facing some challenging stretches ahead. We will need to be reminded that God is good, that God is with us, and that the sacrifices the journey will require of us are more than worth it for the sake of our increasing union with this good and creative and joyful God.

Now the quest can truly begin. It's time to hit the Road.

Bearings

- *Location*: First Threshold > borderland of the darkness of God > "See"
- *Key Concepts*: human as mirror; human essence as relationship with God; God the Son as divine Image; natural unity—essential unity (soul, essence), unity of the spirit (mind: memory, intellect, will), unity of the heart (body); supernatural adornment
- *Practice*: celebration

5

Quest for the Heart

The Journey of the Sun

People in flight along 66. And the concrete road shone like a mirror
under the sun. . . . The people in flight from the terror behind—strange
things happen to them, some bitterly cruel and some so beautiful that
the faith is refired forever.

—John Steinbeck, *The Grapes of Wrath*

WHAT IS A JOURNEY without the Road? In a word: nonexistent. Also:
boring, safe, and uneventful. There is no journey, no adventure, unless we eventually set out. Some of us might prefer it that way—no journey,
no adventure, no setting out. We could stay in the safety of the world as
we've always known it, and we'd stay as we've always been. We could keep
safely studying virtues in the school of the kingdom of the soul, and we'd
probably become legalists. We could even retreat forever into unknowing
and the dark embrace of resting in God, and we'd most likely become isolated mystics. If we refuse the call of the Road, the journey remains incomplete . . . and so do we.

The Road we're called to is not just a fun road trip (though there's
plenty of adventure to be had on those). No, this is a quest, a heroic journey
of transformation. Like Jake and Elwood Blues, we're on a mission from
God. We're looking for more to life. We're looking for more to ourselves.
We're looking for a treasure, a pearl of great price, a kingdom and full life

with its King. What we're looking for specifically—our Object of Search—is the coming of our Bridegroom in this crucial leg of our journey, the Inner Life. And if we're going to find what we're looking for—*who* we're looking for—then we have to follow the Road.

If we're honest, this is the part of the story that makes most of us a little uneasy. The helper must usually be left behind or else goes off on another mission. The group—like Dorothy and her companions, or Frodo and the Fellowship of the Ring, or Luke and his rebel band—often splits up. The strength in numbers is diminished and the hero usually has to go it alone. There are life-changing experiences and insights, but they are likely unrecognized—at least at first—because of the struggle they require. There are trials ahead, maybe monsters of one kind or another, certainly disruptions and threats to safety and the status quo. As John of the Cross explains, "The world, the devil, and the flesh are always in opposition to the journey along this road."[1] But the obstacles and enemies must be faced. This is why we've come. This is our quest.

We remember our mystical earworm: "See, the bridegroom comes! Go out to meet him!" We have already come to understand what we are to "See" in the Inner Life, which is our life as naturally united with God and supernaturally adorned with God's grace and divine essence. Now our quest is to recognize how "the bridegroom comes" to us in the Inner Life, and to "go out" from ourselves in preparation for the eventual "meeting." Here in the Inner Life, Reverend John combines those two elements from his motif, forming what scholar Bernard McGinn calls Ruusbroec's basic law of motion, which says that the movement of the Bridegroom *coming into* us must be matched by our *going out* to him (and to others).[2] As we'll see, this non-dualistic idea of simultaneous inflowing, resting, and outflowing is very important for Ruusbroec (and for us!).

As the coming of Christ in the Active Life was recognized in three ways (past, present, and future), so in the Inner Life Christ's coming happens in three ways: 1) in the heart and bodily faculties; 2) in the spirit and higher faculties of the mind; and 3) in the essential origin, dwelling place, and destination of the soul. These "locations" of Christ's coming and our going out should sound familiar, as they form the theological anthropology—the makeup of the human—that we discussed in the last chapter.

---

1. John of the Cross, *Dark Night*, 1.2.
2. McGinn, *Varieties of Vernacular Mysticism*, 39.

So, just as the "magic mirror" of God turned out to be us, so the Road upon which we'll undertake our quest is within us as well. We are on our way to the deepest parts of our own being. But this is not simple self-improvement. This is regeneration and transformation from the inside out. Our quests will take us deep within because it just so happens that Christ the Bridegroom is also on his way to the deepest parts of our being.

The Journey of the Sun

The first coming of Christ in the Inner Life is in *the heart*. This largely consists of our bodily life—our strengths and weaknesses, the appetites and desires that drive us and sometimes control us. Reverend John likens this stretch of the Road to the shining power of the sun. He uses the cycle of the sun, including astrological signs, to describe our encounter with Christ the Bridegroom. This imagery was characteristic of medieval sensibilities, which were concerned with systems and order. As C. S. Lewis explains, "In medieval science the fundamental concept was that of certain sympathies, antipathies, and strivings inherent in matter itself. Everything has its right place. . . . Besides movement, the spheres transmit (to the Earth) what are called Influences—the subject-matter of Astrology."[3] Though most orthodox medieval theologians like Ruusbroec generally accepted the effects of celestial bodies on events, psychology, and especially plants and minerals, the church fought against resultant beliefs like determinism (believing that events and our own will are out of our hands) and "planetolatry" (worshiping celestial bodies). Here, however, Ruusbroec's use of astrology is chiefly metaphorical and a narrative device.

So, the first stretch of our road trip will be a journey through our heart (our bodily, sensory life), which we'll call the Journey of the Sun. The role of Helper shifts a bit to the more subtle guidance of the Holy Spirit, which is notably different from our more "active" experience of Christ as Helper. Now we focus more on Christ as our Bridegroom, which, as we'll see, is a more exalted and elusive experience of the Second Person of the Trinity. Of course Christ as Helper and Christ as Bridegroom are one and the same, yet they seem somehow different, perhaps in the way Jesus of Nazareth seemed noticeably different from the resurrected Christ (see Luke 24:15–16; John 20:14). We experience the coming of the Bridegroom in the heart and our going out to him in four ways, and each is accompanied by a trial.

3. Lewis, *Discarded Image*, 92, 109.

Encounter One: Fired Up

Our first encounter with the Bridegroom in the heart is characterized by *enkindling and enlightening*—getting fired up, we might say. Our journey begins in late spring on a mountaintop in the highlands, where the sun "produces an earlier summer and many good fruits and strong wine and a land full of joy."[4] Christ, the eternal sun, enlightens and enkindles our sensible faculties. These are the bodily powers, our senses and our appetites and desires, which the Bridegroom's coming draws upward toward higher unity with God. Basically we feel that Christ is with us and we are fired up about getting our bodily life in line with God and God's plan for us.

Our going out to Christ here consists of five attitudes or movements in response to this coming:

1. Singleness of heart, which is an inward attention to our bodily faculties

2. Inner practice, a conscious turning inward to understand God working in us

3. Sensible affection, which replaces all competing affections with a yearning, savoring desire for God

4. Devotedness of our bodily life to God and God's glory, which opens the straight path of blessedness

5. Thanksgiving and praise, which is the appropriate disposition of the devoted, inner person

This is all something like a "mountaintop experience," in which we feel close to God and are ready to seize the day. Christ's presence within us excites us to play host to him, to do all we can to make the sort of bodily life in which Christ is at home.

However, as we enjoy this spiritual high, we soon encounter our first trial: a feeling of frustration and woe at our insufficiency in light of God's goodness. The initial God-high begins to give way to a recognition of the differences and seeming distance between us. Our thanks, praise, honor, and service are not enough. Our growth in charity, virtues, faithfulness, and godliness is insufficient. We might try to manufacture more such experiences to keep our warm feelings going, but we cannot fake our way through this quest. It's as if we are at a party and we look around and realize that the guest of honor, God, has left. We feel all fired up with no place to

---

4. John of Ruusbroec, *Spiritual Espousals*, b192–93.

go. It seemed okay at first, kind of like a religious pep rally—all the excitement of the game without any challenge or struggle . . . or growth or chance for victory. We can stay put and pretend, or we can resume our quest. This is our first trial.

Interestingly, our encounters with Christ in the heart are incomplete without the trials. This is to say, Christ uses the enkindling and enlightening of the mountaintop experience to produce the woe of insufficiency. The point is not the spiritual high but the longing for more of the God who produces it. We aren't fired up for the pep rally but for the game. Like the drawn-out humidity and blossoming and fruitfulness that characterize late spring, Reverend John analogizes, so Christ the sun draws heat from earthly things, causes the heart to grow and leaf with inner affection, to blossom with yearning and devotion, to produce fruit with thanks and praise, and to preserve the fruit eternally in humble woe from "perpetual want."[5] Basically, it seems everything around us and within us is awakening us to God. And this blooming is not for its own sake, but for a fragrant offering to God.

We should pause here to focus in on this trial of "perpetual want." It is a vital concept in the mystic way known as *epektasis*, which is something like insatiable hunger. Others have written about *epektasis*. For example, the Cappadocian (in modern Turkey) mystical theologian Gregory of Nyssa (ca. 335–ca. 395) explored it in his *Life of Moses*, explaining that "what Moses yearned for is satisfied by the very things which leave his desire unsatisfied."[6] Moses's mystical mountaintop encounters with God stirred a deep longing that kept him wanting more. Later, medieval mystic and shrewd reformer Bernard of Clairvaux (1090–1153) explained that "even when it has found [God] the soul will not cease to seek him," because "what is desired does not end desire but extends it . . . it is oil poured on flames, which itself catches fire."[7] Bernard posited that this unquenchable desire continues even in heaven. This is not because God is unsatisfying, of course, but because God is inexhaustible—the more we taste, the more we want to taste.

So, Reverend John presents it here as our first trial, the woe of perpetual want: our experience of God is destined to leave us wanting more.

---

5. John of Ruusbroec, *Spiritual Espousals*, b307.

6. Gregory of Nyssa, *Vit. Mos.* 2.235.

7. Bernard of Clairvaux, "Sermons," 84.1.

And like many trials, it is a blessing in disguise. After all, the longing is what keeps our journey going.

Encounter Two: Spiritually Drunk

Our second encounter with the Bridegroom in the heart produces *sweetness and spiritual drunkenness.* The Journey of the Sun reaches the transition from spring to summer, characterized by the sign of Gemini, the twin, for the sun has double strength on growing things, as it draws out moisture and produces dew and rain, resulting in fruitfulness. Here, Christ the sun is raised up in the heart above all things. We become more mature and discerning about the demands of bodily appetites that oppose the spirit, which are now becoming well ordered and under control. Our enjoyment and rest in practicing the virtuous life are directed to God by the warmth of active love. The result is the "sweet rain of new inward blessing and heavenly dew of divine sweetness."[8] It's like when we learn a new word and then start hearing and seeing it all over the place. Or perhaps it is more like the early stages of falling in love. Our newfound devotion and dedication of our bodily life to Christ results in recognizing Christ within us and all around us.

Our response is to go out in a double (twin) increase in virtues, which in turn results in a new experience of the coming of Christ. Here is a back-and-forth of experiences of Christ's coming and our going out. His presence makes us want to do better, to be better. The sweetness of his coming results in a blissfulness of heart and all the bodily faculties. Increasingly, what we see and hear, what we smell and taste, what we touch and feel, all of our bodily life seems to be caught up in the goodness of creation. There is a feeling of being enfolded in a divine embrace.

From this bliss comes what Reverend John calls a spiritual drunkenness, in which our heart overflows with an overwhelming feeling of enjoyment and wellbeing. This experience might even be characterized by any number of ecstatic responses, such as singing, getting tearful, moving through the day with a spring in our step and even dancing and clapping and cheering, awestruck silence, and the mixed feeling that everyone is sharing this experience and, at the same time, that no one else knows such fullness.

8. John of Ruusbroec, *Spiritual Espousals*, b324.

Along with this sweetness and spiritual drunkenness, we experience our next (twin) trials: an overestimation of ourselves and an overreliance on our blessings. Like hoarfrost overtaking blossoms and depriving their fruitfulness, we are tempted to overestimate our deservedness of blessing, possibly developing a sense of entitlement toward God. And, like haze descending on the Road and clouding our journey, we can become overly reliant on the feeling of sweetness and inner blessings, which can cloud our thinking. We might even give ourselves over to a manufactured false sweetness, which, like the empty attempts to stay fired up, can deviate us from the journey and even from God.

So, these trials teach us humility in recognizing that our blissful feelings and blessings and even the virtues we respond with are not the result of our deservedness. All of it is only the result of God's gracious generosity within us and around us.

Encounter Three: Wounded by Love

Our third encounter with the Bridegroom coming in our heart is characterized by *yearning with desire and joy*. The sun is at its highest point, in Cancer, the crab, in which the sun cannot advance higher but, like a crab, begins to go backwards. This is the hottest and driest time of year. Likewise, Christ is raised up in our heart to the highest point, above all blessings, gifts, or sweetness.

The result is a growing self-mastery. We turn back inward in humble praise and thanks toward the divine Ground from whom all gifts flow. Christ is exalted in our heart and wants to draw all things to himself, namely, all our bodily faculties (senses, appetites, and abilities). We yearn to surpass all blessings and gifts and simply to find our Beloved. We experience Christ calling us to overcome any attachment to our own life and experiences of bodily blessing and to be joined only to him, our Bridegroom.

This back-and-forth experience of Christ demanding more of us, and our yearning to give it, constitutes a crucial trial, in which we are wounded by the "lacerations of love."[9] Reverend John describes our heart's desperate struggle to reach unity with its Beloved. From this inability either to obtain God or to go without God comes a feeling of agitation and restlessness, both inside and out. It's the stuff of countless poems and love songs, the frustrated longing for the beloved. I can't live with or without you.

9. John of Ruusbroec, *Spiritual Espousals*, b424–25.

This inner affliction is characterized by a willingness "to suffer all that can be suffered in order to obtain what one loves," to the extent that this agitation "eats a person's heart and drinks his blood."[10] Such graphic imagery illustrates the depth of our struggle to overcome our divided, creaturely nature at odds with itself, and also the depth of our *pathos* and the increasing desire for union with our Beloved.[11] This "laceration of love" is a typical experience on the hero's journey, in which the hero is branded or receives a wound (certainly inner, if not also outer) as the result of a struggle.[12] It is an experience of atonement, of participating in Christ's passion and death— being "crucified with Christ" (Gal 2:20)—giving way to new life with God.[13] It is our heart's openness and yearning that results in its woundedness. It is no wonder, then, that this trial is both sweet and painful, at once an injury and a sign of our healing, and resulting in both wealth and woe.

The journey through this third heart-encounter with Christ continues into the deep summertime, marked by Leo the lion, which has a violent nature since he is lord over the animals. Here, our bodily nature is consumed, sometimes replaced by a yearning to be released from the body as if from a prison. We might think of the heavenly hall of glory full of unending joy and rapturous worship, and be grieved to tears with the feeling that our brokenness and bodily appetites leave us in a sort of exile. This stage might even be characterized by visions, revelations, and rapture, in which we have inexplicable glimpses into our own spirit like lightning flashes. Like the dog days of late summer with their drawn-out heat and dryness, so we experience the rash and restless heat of affection and yearning. We are like a woman in labor unable to deliver.

Once again, however, our trials are our blessings. If we will respond to our yearning and agitation and restlessness with continued discipline and worship and virtues, these trials become the very things that keep us going

10. John of Ruusbroec, *Spiritual Espousals*, b446–49.

11. Literary theorist Northrop Frye describes the stages of the romantic quest "using the Greek terms, the *agon* or conflict, the *pathos* or death-struggle, and the *anagnorisis* or discovery, the recognition of the hero, who has clearly proved himself to be a hero even if he does not survive the conflict." Frye, *Anatomy of Criticism*, 187. These stages parallel the stages of Ruusbroec's spiritual path.

12. Propp, *Morphology of the Folktale*, 52.

13. See Joseph Campbell on "Atonement with the Father" in the hero's journey, and specifically the example of Christ's atonement, in Campbell, *Hero with Thousand Faces*, 120.

and drawing ever closer to God. We know that relief will be found only in the eventual deeper meeting with our Bridegroom.

Encounter Four: Desolate Joy

Our fourth, and final, encounter with Christ our Bridegroom coming in our heart is characterized by *the deep joy of desolation*. This final leg of the Journey of the Sun occurs at the end of summertime, in the sign called Virgo, because this season becomes unfruitful like a virgin. It is in this season that the virgin Mary is said to have gone to heaven full of joy and rich from all virtues. This combination of unfruitfulness with fullness of joy and riches will characterize the final stretch of this quest. Basically the mountaintop experiences are long gone, and we're okay with that.

Following the intense heat of the last encounter, with Christ the sun in the zenith of our heart, now comes a waning and cooling, with Christ hiding and withdrawing his interior shining. Following this manner of coming (by seemingly going), Christ again calls us to go out to him. Going out, however, we find ourselves poor, miserable, and even feeling forsaken. All the sweetness of inner blessing, joy, and sensible enjoyment that characterized the earlier encounters are gone. Even the fierce agitation of love that so tormented us previously is now missed. Here we stand . . . alone.

This is another level of John of the Cross's "dark night," in which he says God's grace is like a loving mother who "sets her child down from her arms, letting it walk on its own feet so that it may put aside the habits of childhood and grow accustomed to greater and more important things."[14] As we are perhaps beginning to recognize, this encounter with the Bridegroom is also the trial, and a serious trial it is. Can our bodies withstand the denial of the sweet milk of gifts and ecstasies and walk on into the promise of more deeply satisfying nourishment?

Despite the poverty and suffering of this experience of desolation, we can still find satisfaction and even joy and gladness here. In fact, if we will stay on track and keep pursuing God above all else, we will never have tasted joy so deep. Nothing is more delightful to the lover of God than to feel that we belong to God, and that this belonging is enough. It might seem strange if compared to our earlier experiences of pep rally faith and drunken spirituality, but what keeps us going now is humble obedience in devotion and patient forsakenness in suffering.

14. John of the Cross, *Dark Night*, 1.1.2.

Presumably the consolation in the midst of this desolation is the result of awareness of the journey itself. We must carefully reengage with Reason to maintain our bearings and continue on the journey, despite the lack of felt blessings and spiritual highs. This is a season of spiritual lows, which are the result of traveling to new depths in our heart's connection to God, which is to say the body as the location of divine encounter. We find solace in stepping back, considering our journey, and pressing on.

Our quest now continues into Libra, the scales, in which day and night stand in balance as the sun deals out light against the darkness. Likewise, Christ stands in balance with us in our apparent forsakenness. Whatever comes, whether sweet or bitter, we now are able to accept equally (except sin, which is to be driven out altogether). It is harvest time. All the inward and outward virtues we ever practiced are offered to God like the ripe fruits of the harvest. Because of our desolate state, says Reverend John, the harvest fruits of virtue are far more precious to God: "Thus the virtues are fulfilled, and desolation becomes eternal wine."[15] Those people who are close to us at this stage are enriched and edified by our virtuous life and patient endurance, and like scattered grain, our virtues are sowed and multiplied for the benefit of others.

Is this enough for us? How long can we continue giving without getting for ourselves? At this point in his narrative, Reverend John presents a warning about the vulnerability of this state of what he calls our forsakenness. As this is the season of the equinox when the sun sets early and the weather gets cool, so those who lack strength in adversity find the weather within them becoming cool, resulting in evil humors.

As C. S. Lewis explains of medieval thought, there are many ways in which the human body is a microcosm of the larger creation, and the governing presence of humors is a prime example.[16] The so-called "four contraries" that combine in the greater world to form the elements of fire, air, water, and earth, also combine in the human body to form the humors: "Hot and Moist make Blood; Hot and Dry, Choler; Cold and Moist, Phlegm; Cold and Dry, Melancholy. . . . The proportion in which the Humours are blended differs from one man to another and constitutes his *complexion* or *temperamentum*, his combination or mixture."[17] Blood was associated

15. John of Ruusbroec, *Spiritual Espousals*, b648–49.

16. See Lewis, *Discarded Image*, 169–74.

17. Lewis, *Discarded Image*, 170. Lewis also notes, "In addition to this permanent predominance of some one Humour in each individual, there is also a daily rhythmic

with being sanguine, i.e., enthusiastic and active; choler (yellow bile) with being irritable and angry; melancholy (black bile) with being preoccupied and somewhat neurotic (a bit different from the modern understanding of "melancholy" as introspective and sad); and phlegm with being reserved and even unemotional and dull.

This might sound to us like outdated superstition and ignorance about human physiology. However, this is far from the case, and we have much to learn here. As has been true of the spiritual "weather" on our Journey of the Sun, the order here moves from better to worse, which is to say the "hot" humors are preferred to the "cold." Reverend John develops a lengthy description of the various states or "illnesses" that result from the cooling, evil humors that lead many astray in this season of the journey.

There are certain characteristics of such cooling that we are wise to watch out for. We might find ourselves with an increasing desire for outward things and earthly comfort. We might become distracted and preoccupied with worldly things. This can lead to instability and fickleness about the things of God. It might even lead to alienation from God, from self, from truth, and from virtues. Eventually we become apathetic and negligent toward everything needed for eternal life, which is to say the life of God and with God. We might abandon the journey altogether.

It might surprise us to discover that, despite our growth and maturity, we can come this far on the journey and yet, as Reverend John says, still walk upon the brink of hell and fall into sins like someone who never knew God. It is vital to recognize that, even in the deeper stages of the journey, our quest to be joined to our Bridegroom is always threatened by our own sin-inclined, creaturely nature. It is essential, then, that we constantly "offer [our] bodies as a living sacrifice, holy and pleasing to God—this is [our] true and proper worship" (Rom 12:1), which is exactly what this particular quest through the heart has been about.

In contrast to our tendency toward waywardness, we do well here to return to the lessons of Christ our Helper, who has already successfully navigated this entire Journey of the Sun. The sweetness, consolation, and virtues, as well as the trials, wounds, and forsakenness, all find their perfection in Christ. He knows what it is to bring the heart—the senses and desires and bodily appetites, the strengths and vulnerabilities—into complete

---

variation which gives each of the four a temporary predominance in all of us. Blood is dominant from midnight till 6 a.m.; Choler, from then till noon; Melancholy, from noon till 6 p.m.; then Phlegm till midnight. (All this, it should be remembered, is geared for people who got up and went to bed far earlier than we.)" Lewis, *Discarded Image*, 173.

devotion, submission, and love to God. To undertake the Journey of the Sun is only to follow in Christ's footsteps, and to go out to that Bridegroom who comes to us.

Way-Stop #5: Reflection

So, with our eyes on Christ our forerunner, we come to the completion of this quest through the heart. We have cooperated with God's work of purging our hearts of competing affections and allegiances, and we arrive to find God shining and warming us within. The quest has led us from desires and appetites for the things of the world, to desires and appetites for the things of God, and now to desires and appetites for God alone. It is certainly true that as long as our body is with us, its appetites are with us as well. But we should be beginning to experience our bodily existence as both a location of and a means for experiencing the fuller life of God, refusing the many poor worldly imitations and substitutes.

Fasting is an especially helpful practice here, reminding us that we do "not live on bread alone, but on every word that comes from the mouth of God" (Matt 4:4). We should not think of fasting as merely abstaining from food but as redirecting our appetites toward God alone. We might set aside one specific day each week and fast through one meal, and in a few weeks try fasting from lunch to lunch or sundown to sundown. We should sustain ourselves with water and break the fast with fresh fruits and vegetables and maybe broth. We might work our way up to longer fasts, but we should never call undue attention to our fasting. It is a precious means of sharing in God's grace, not a feat of spiritual strength, and it creates space in our bodies as our meeting place with God.

There's one more thing about the completion of this quest and our present arrival in God's sunny company. With a wink and a smile, Reverend John lets us in on a little secret: we could have experienced this illumination all at once at the beginning of this quest, but the journey was necessary for us to actually realize it. Since we are both naturally united with God and now supernaturally adorned with God's grace, it isn't as if we are becoming *more* one with God. We are simply living more and more into oneness.

We'll have more to say on this later. For now it's enough to say that the quests are completely necessary. For example, now we have a much fuller understanding of, appreciation for, and mastery over our divinely adorned heart and bodily life united with God. This is true of coming quests, that

God could impart their transformative lessons to us at the very beginning. But that is of no matter. Magical makeovers and quick fixes are fine, but they are never as deeply transformative as the blessings and trials of life itself, especially life with God. It's a lesson of the Road.

Bearings

- *Location*: the Road > the Inner Life > "the bridegroom comes; go out" in the heart (body)
- *Key Concepts*: the heart as bodily life; enkindling and enlightening (fired up); *epektasis*; sweetness and spiritual drunkenness; yearning with desire and joy; wounds of love; atonement; deep joy of desolation; cooling humors
- *Practice*: fasting

6

Quest for the Spirit

The Journey of the Streams

Sometimes we'd have that whole river all to ourselves for the longest
time. Yonder was the banks and the islands, across the water; and maybe
a spark—which was a candle in a cabin window—and sometimes on
the water you could see a spark or two—on a raft or a scow, you know;
and maybe you could hear a fiddle or a song coming from one of them
crafts. It's lovely to live on a raft.

—Mark Twain, *The Adventures of Huckleberry Finn*

H AVING TRAVELED FOR MONTHS and seasons of sun cycles—from
springtime fruitfulness to summertime drought to autumn harvest—the Road now leads us to a system of streams. As with Odysseus,
Captain Ahab, Huckleberry Finn, "old man" Santiago, Dory and Nemo
and so many others, our quest requires us to take to the water. Water is a
fascinating setting for an adventure. It's both life-giving and threatening.
It's navigable and chaotic. It's liberating and imprisoning. It gently cradles
us as we drift along almost weightless, while dark depths and mysterious
creatures lurk under the surface with the potential to pull us down. And all
of this makes water a most appropriate setting for a journey through the
mind and a quest for the spirit.

For us, however, this quest is the place where our white whales are set
free into an infinitely larger ocean. Whatever preoccupations or obsessions

we have—about ourselves, about our culture and our world, about reality itself—here become figures growing ever smaller behind us as we sail in a different direction. Though they might pursue us in the deep like Leviathan, or entice us toward the rocks like the Sirens, our mental fixations and misguided ways of answering the questions of more to life and more to ourselves have no place in these waters.

The Journey of the Streams

As we recall our theological anthropology, we remember that humans are fundamentally a relationship with God. Each of us is naturally united with God in our heart (strength, our bodily appetites and abilities), in our spirit (mind, our thoughts and feelings), and in our essence (soul, our aliveness both in ourselves and in God). We need this triple unity in order to exist as humans. However, this "natural unity" is not enough for us to fully participate in the life and love of God, to fulfill Jesus's command to love God and others with our whole being. For that, each of these unities must be "supernaturally adorned," which is to say they must be surrendered and subjected to God's transforming grace. As a result, the "magic mirror" of our life as God's image comes to more and more faithfully reflect God. Bit by bit, we become like God. Having completed (though it's forever ongoing) the quest for the heart, with our bodily life and desires now set on God alone, we turn to the quest for the spirit.

This is the second "coming" of Christ the Bridegroom in this second leg of the journey, the Inner Life, which we are considering in terms of a Road story. In his narrative, Reverend John likens this second manner of Christ the Bridegroom's coming to three streams that spring up from a fountain and run through us. Like a deep well, the fullness of God's grace dwells within us. And like streams bursting forth, God's grace actively flows out into our "spirit," which should be understood as our mind with its three higher faculties: memory (mindfulness), understanding (reason), and will (drive).

Though we will continue to experience trials and the purging of worldly and creaturely inclinations, the journey here shifts from the so-called "way of purgation" (*via purgativa*) to the "way of illumination" (*via illuminativa*), as we might expect in moving from a quest characterized by scorching heat and desolation to a quest characterized by refreshing streams. Where the unity of the heart was about offering our bodies as a living sacrifice, this unity of the spirit is about being "transformed by the renewing of your minds. Then you will be able to test and approve what God's will is—his good, pleasing and perfect will" (Rom 12:2). This is a quest to learn how to think.[1]

One: The Stream of Memory

The first stream we encounter flows from the fountain of God's grace into the spirit/mind and produces *simplicity in the memory*. By "memory" Reverend John seems to mean our faculty for self-reflection, mindfulness, or self-awareness. This is more present-oriented than the modern understanding of "memory" with its focus almost totally on the past. However, there is an element of considering the ways our past has shaped our thinking, especially about ourselves, our world, and what is real. We might think in terms of *recollection*, of gathering disparate thoughts and attitudes—likely including some from the past—and focusing them and simplifying them in the living present. This stream carries our thinking beyond the many sensory images standing on the riverbanks, distractions that haunt us like ghosts in our mind's recesses . . . or sometimes appear front and center.

It's as if Christ our Bridegroom arrives with a boat and carries us from the chaotic mainland into a calming stream, which is the awareness that our spirit is actually one, not many. This really can be a helpful mental exercise, whether in a time of meditation or engaged in the day's activities: We imagine the regrets of the past or distractions of the present or fears of the future as figures standing on a riverbank, and we climb into a boat with Jesus and drift away on the stream of focused awareness, of simplified mindfulness.

This mindfulness says that we are not the many roles the world has tried to cast us in, not the deformed creatures we or others have tried to make of us, not the many personas we've tried on or hidden behind. We possess a dynamic core that forms us into a person. And that core is singular and unique. Each of us is one person, beheld by and beloved of God, "an unceasing spiritual being with an eternal destiny in God's good universe."[2]

---

1. We should remember that this is not simply about our brain functions, but about our thinking and feeling that connect to and shape our life both within and beyond our body. This is why it is called "spirit."

2. This is Dallas Willard's characterization, found, for example, in Willard, *Divine Conspiracy*, 21, 86.

This revelation is what is meant by "simplicity of memory," which is to say an undistracted focus on our true self united with God.

The enlightening simplicity of this stream of Christ the Bridegroom's coming in grace prompts us to "go out." Such going out is actually a turning inward, focusing the memory on bareness above sensory distractions. Our life is not defined by all the noise and images and information around us and inside us. Instead, we are one: one with ourselves and one with God. This simplicity of focus is fundamentally for the sake of possessing, of living into, this dynamic core of our beloved personhood. To "go out" here is to live mindfully in light of the fact that our mind—with all its thoughts and feelings—is grounded in God and supernaturally adorned within us. We are gifted with personhood and graced with true self-awareness.

This mindfulness is our own dwelling place and the eternal and personal inheritance of our true self. The life of the mind, including all that is meant by our true self-awareness, should constantly be informed by our simple and eternal unity with God. This is a *detachment* from the dictates of sensory distractions, and a deeper *attachment* to (unity with) the fountain of God's grace, from which this first stream flows through our spirit: simplicity of memory.

Two: The Stream of Understanding

As we navigate the tranquil waters of simplicity of memory, the stream forks off into another stream: *clarity of understanding*. The fullness of God's grace in the unity of our spirit overflows into a stream of spiritual clarity that flows and shines in our understanding (intellect, reason). We can imagine the sun dancing on the water around us, which sparkles like a bed of diamonds. The waters of our mind that are so often churned up and muddy with distractions and preoccupations, here God calms and illumines, revealing the life and world within.

Reverend John reminds us that this illumination is dependent on God, who can offer or withhold the light according to God's will. At this stage, however, we are content either way, having transcended the need for sensory stimulation and set all our affections on God and God's good will. Nevertheless, as Christ the Bridegroom comes and shines with clarity in our understanding, he calls us to "go out" and walk—or perhaps swim—in this light.

This clarity of understanding enables us to go out from ourselves and examine our state and our life within and without, especially considering our likeness to Christ and how faithfully we are reflecting God's image. We can recall how, in the Active Life, the threshold guardian of Reason had to be overcome by love and longing for God alone. We had to trust the unseen and let go of our need to overanalyze and control. But here, in the Inner Life, God's overflowing grace empowers us to lift up our enlightened eyes and see the truth, to employ our now enlightened Reason in examining and beholding God's exalted nature and fathomless attributes. Instead of trying to figure out and manipulate God, we are now able and content to simply behold God and respond with appropriate awe and love.

As we drift along these waters of clear understanding, our mind's eye begins to take in the life of the Godhead (which is to say God as One, the divine Unity) and the divine Persons (God as Three, the divine Trinity). Reverend John, our guide, describes the nature of the Godhead in spatial terms, as "inaccessible height, and unfathomable depth, incomprehensible breadth and eternal length, a dark stillness and a wild desert."[3] Rather than rushing on, we should dwell upon this description of the divine Unity, the life of God as One: a mountain so tall that its summit can never be reached; an ocean so deep that its bottom can never be touched; a landscape so vast that it can be endlessly traveled and explored; the still simplicity of a dark night; the untamed beauty of a pristine wilderness. The more time we spend taking it in, the more our enlightened Reason clarifies and illumines the limitless landscape of the divine nature, though we are just as powerless as we ever were to comprehend it all.

Reverend John moves from the Godhead to each respective divine Person—Father, Son, Holy Spirit—pointing out some of their character- istics. The Father is almighty power and majesty, the creator and sustainer and mover, the beginning and end, the cause of all that is. The Son is the eternal Word, unfathomable wisdom and truth, the perfect exemplar of all creatures, the eternal and unchangeable rule, the penetrating vision of all things. The Holy Spirit is incomprehensible love and generosity, compas- sion and graciousness, faithfulness and goodness flowing through us—a blazing flame, a flowing fountain, our introduction into our eternal bless- edness, and the embrace of the Father and the Son and all of us in joyful union. Each divine Person lives distinct from the others, and yet they all move and come together as one.

3. John of Ruusbroec, *Spiritual Espousals*, b891–93.

Such a view of the eternal landscape of the Godhead and the divine Persons results in an understandable state of awe. Especially welcome after traversing the hot wasteland and trials of the heart in the Journey of the Sun, this stream of God's grace has carried us to a glimpse of the promised land of our true life in God. Our astonishment results from the rush of understanding that God is all and yet particular to each of us, for through God all things exist, and in God and on God hang heaven and earth and all aspects of being. Yet God is fully within each of us, uniquely knowing us and loving us.

Though many fall away on the inner journey, those of us who reach this clarity of understanding are rewarded with an inward joy of the spirit and a great confidence in God. How could we feel otherwise, considering this vision of such a dazzling reality? Here is the profound truth of the words of early church father Irenaeus of Lyons (ca. 130–ca. 200): the glory of God is a human fully alive; and life consists in beholding God.[4] And here is new meaning to the old song: Row, row, row your boat gently down the stream; merrily, merrily, merrily, merrily, life is but a dream. This mind's-eye glimpse of the unseen divine reality behind all things puts our petty distractions and preoccupations in their place, offering a deep clarity of understanding.

Three: The Stream of the Will

Now the two streams we've navigated—simplicity of memory and clarity of understanding—come together into a third stream: *an enkindled will.* "Will" here indicates what drives us to do what we do, to become the sort of person we're becoming. So, the simplified awareness of our true self united with God, and the clarified understanding of our life embraced in the eternal divine Unity and Trinity, both come together to fire us up to become more and more that true self, to better and better understand that divine Unity and Trinity with whom we share life. In short, we *will* to think and live as one with God.

In the end, this is what we get out of our life and what we have to show for ourselves, namely, the kind of person we've become and are becoming. As Dallas Willard explains, "The intention of God is that we should each become the kind of person whom he can set free in his universe, empowered

---

4. Irenaeus, *Ag. Haer.* 4.20.7.

to do what *we* want to do."[5] That might surprise us. After all, isn't God's aim for us to do what *God* wants us to do? This consideration hinges on our growing understanding of God and our true selves. Do we really think the Father of Jesus, the God who is Love, is set on programming us like machines or training us like animals? No, our divine Parent wants nothing more than for us to grow and mature into free eternal beings that can will and work creatively in our own way as unique bearers of God's image.

This should also shed some light on the question of God's will for our life, which is often the source of panic and regret when it should be the source of childlike curiosity and joy. Many of us make the mistake of thinking of God's will for us as a set of hidden blueprints that must be discovered and followed exactly, with tragic consequences if we miss even one stroke. Instead, it would seem that it's all more like an empty journal or huge canvas, on which we're invited to work with God in writing the story or painting the picture we envision together. And if we mess it up, there's grace to start again. In time—years, decades, centuries, millennia—we might really start getting somewhere. But for now, we begin with our will.

This stream of the will pulls the other streams into itself, with the simplicity of our mindfulness and clarity of our understanding contributing to the stirring of our will. In the words of Curly, the grizzled but beloved old cowboy in *City Slickers*, the meaning of life is "one thing," which is for us to figure out. For those of us on this journey, though our chosen expressions of that one thing are as unique as each of us, in the bigger picture that one thing is union: we live for and from our true selves as one with God. As Søren Kierkegaard explains in his fittingly titled work, *Purity of Heart Is to Will One Thing*, "A collected mind is a mind that has collected itself from every distraction, from every relation, in order to center itself upon this relation to itself as an individual who is responsible to God. It is a mind that has collected itself from every distraction, and therefore also from all comparison."[6] Here is something of a sketch of this Journey of the Streams: a collected mind, freed from distractions, centered on itself as an individual, and responsible to God.

Union with God, then, must become our mental North Star guiding our journey from here on. Reverend John says that our enkindled will is "like a fire" that "devours and consumes everything in unity."[7] All our other

5. Willard, *Divine Conspiracy*, 379 (emphasis original).

6. Kierkegaard, *Purity of Heart*, 216.

7. John of Ruusbroec, *Spiritual Espousals*, b958.

life projects must be burned to the ground for the sake of experiencing God's abundant and eternal life growing and budding in their place. Now we do what we do and are becoming who we're becoming only for the sake of life with God. Anything that gets in the way of this—any mental boulders or debris that disrupt the flow of this stream—must be removed.

The stream of our will drives all aspects of our life. It flows through all our faculties—heart and body, spirit and mind, soul and essence—and pulls us like a current. It sets the course for the kind of person we're becoming, either drawing us toward the riverbank of the world and all its distractions and pitfalls and chaos, or toward the heights and depths and vast expanse of the life of God. When we set ourselves to "go out" to Christ the Bridegroom and to move with his eternal current, Reverend John says it is then that we become "a spiritually enlightened person."[8]

With the completion of this quest and leg of our journey, we are indeed on course to become the kind of person God can set free and empower to do what *we* want to do in God's good universe. This is not to be taken lightly. This, after all, is the goal of this quest for the spirit and journey through the mind. Simplicity. Clarity. Fire.

Way-Stop #6: Reflection

There are many books and tools concerned with renewing the mind. We've probably encountered and even employed a few of them. Perhaps some were helpful and some were a waste of time. However, what the bulk of them miss is this focus on our connectedness to God, our place in the divine landscape. They might help us replace bad thoughts with good or even attain a healthier understanding and view of ourselves. But what they rarely or never do is open our minds to our true selves as one with the divine Unity and Trinity.

It's like Jesus's parable about the person who sweeps his house clean of all the demonic distractions but fails to fill it with God (Luke 11:24–26). Left empty, the house is soon haunted by even more devilish hangers-on than before. Likewise, it does us no good to employ a bunch of tools in a mind-renewal project if we have no goal for exactly what it is we're building in place of the old, or if we're just replacing the old with cheap, plastic self-help décor instead of total transformation from the foundation up.

8. John of Ruusbroec, *Spiritual Espousals*, b969.

In these three streams—simplicity of memory, clarity of understanding, and enkindled will—our past, present, and future begin to flow together in the eternal now (more on that later). Our thoughts and feelings, our awareness and understanding, what we're about and what drives us, all begin to be redirected so that "we have the mind of Christ" (1 Cor 2:16). This mind is always and simultaneously caught up in outwardly-flowing love with the divine Trinity, inwardly-flowing peace with the divine Unity, and restful joy within the two. So, "let the same mind be in you that was in Christ Jesus" (Phil 2:5 NRSV)—that's what we're striving for.

Meditation can be a helpful practice for keeping our mind aware and clear and kindled. There are many forms of meditation from many different traditions. We've mentioned *lectio divina*, which includes meditative focus on scriptural passages. Also, as we've touched on, breath prayers are an effective way of quieting and focusing the mind by simply repeating or thinking a word or phrase as we inhale and exhale, such as "Abba Father," "Jesus," "Holy Spirit," "Yahweh," "I am with you," or whatever is meaningful to us.[9] (The actual words are less important than repeatedly and fully turning the mind to God.) Memorizing Scripture, whether particular verses or full chapters (don't underestimate yourself!), can also be a way of keeping the mind directed toward God throughout the day and during long, restless nights.

As the journey continues, we come to understand that God's supernatural adornment is not a one-time thing, but is constantly dressing us with grace and empowering us to participate in the life of God. So, as we share in the outward movement of the Triune Persons—Father, Son, and Spirit—we, like Christ, are mediators between God and others, teaching and guiding and serving. We become something like a channel through which these streams of spiritual unity flow into the world around us. However, in keeping with our spiritual "law of motion," these streams that flow outward must also flow back to their Source.

---

9. This manner of meditative prayer is rooted in the *hesychasm* of the Eastern Orthodox tradition. The stages of the practice are familiar and in line with the stages presented in this book: *katharsis* (purgation), *theōria* (illumination), and *theōsis* (union, deification). These "breath prayers" are part of the *theōria* stage, similar to Ruusbroec's present "unity of the spirit" stage, which emphasizes awareness of the presence of God within us. The practice often employs repetition of some form of the Jesus Prayer: "Lord Jesus Christ, Son of God, have mercy on me, a sinner."

Bearings

- *Location*: the Road > the Inner Life > "the bridegroom comes; go out" in the spirit (mind)

- *Key Concepts*: the spirit as mind (thoughts, feelings); the higher faculties of the mind—memory (mindfulness), understanding (intellect, reason), will (drive); *via illuminativa*; simplicity of memory (true self as one); clarity of understanding (embraced in the divine Tri-Unity); enkindled will (fired up and free)

- *Practice*: meditation

7

QUEST FOR THE ESSENCE

The Journey into the Fountain

The old man knew he was going far out and he left the smell of the
land behind and rowed out into the clean early morning smell of the
ocean. He saw the phosphorescence of the Gulf weed in the water as he
rowed over the part of the ocean that the fishermen called the great well
because there was a sudden deep of seven hundred fathoms.

—Ernest Hemingway, *The Old Man and the Sea*

M OST OF US ARE familiar with the phenomenon of the current. If we've
swum in the ocean or some other sizeable body of water, we've likely
had the experience of swimming in one direction and finding ourselves
pulled the opposite way. We might get our bearings by spying our towel
or umbrella on the beach, only to find that, despite being sure we've been
paddling and bobbing in the same spot for a short while, we have drifted far
out of range of our little camp. And anyone who knows this experience also
knows that fighting the current is exhausting and, ultimately, a losing battle.
So, if we want to follow Jesus's instruction to "put out into the deep water"
(Luke 5:4), we must be prepared to let the current carry us a bit.

At this point on our journey we are indeed moving under our own
power into the deeper waters. But we have reached our limit. We keep up
the virtuous practices of the Active Life and we draw on the lessons of the
Inner Life so far, all of which continue to transform our bodily and mental

inclinations. But there's a current that is drawing us in a new direction. Strive as we might, we cannot resist this pull toward something deeper. We might even swim for the shore in an attempt to gain a firmer footing, telling ourselves we're satisfied with the journey so far and we've come far enough.

There is an element of defeat here. Just when it seemed we were making significant progress, we're knocked out of commission. Daniel LaRusso is heading for victory at the All-Valley Karate Championships, only to have Cobra Kai sweep his leg. Aladdin returns from a magic carpet ride having won Jasmine's affection, only to get captured and thrown into the sea. In *The Princess Bride*, Westley is finally reunited with Buttercup only to be arrested and taken to the Pit of Despair. The only way to continue is for the helper to step in. All our training and work have brought us here, but there's only one discipline we've learned that can serve us now: letting go.

The Journey into the Fountain

In one of his more famous and powerful passages, Reverend John explains that the "flowing of God always demands a flowing back, for God is a flowing, ebbing sea, which flows without cease into all his beloved. . . . And He is ebbing back in again, drawing all those whom He has endowed on heaven and earth, together with all that they have and can do."[1] God is ceaselessly flowing into us with God's life and love and God-ness. But that's not the only direction God flows. There is a divine current pulling us back, drawing us into mysterious waters. There's no use fighting it—this is what we've been searching for.

This is the third "coming" of Christ our Bridegroom on the Road through the Inner Life. We followed the sun and seasons on the quest for the heart (body), and the three streams on our quest for the spirit (mind). Now we are pulled back to the fountainhead of those same streams where we are challenged to dive in to reach the living vein that wells up from the ground of God's grace and riches. Here, the streams of the higher faculties of the unity of the spirit (memory, understanding, will) come together and ebb back into their origin. This is the quest for our very essence.

---

1. John of Ruusbroec, *Spiritual Espousals*, b986–91.

Essential Unity and the Divine Touch

This is a new quest and a new experience, yet these are the same waters as the previous unity, the unity of the spirit/mind. However, where that spiritual unity was active, which is to say mostly under our control, here it is passive. At this point, "no one works but God alone, out of free goodness, which is the cause of all our virtues and all our blessedness."[2] This is the source of all grace and gifts, the fountain that wells up and overflows into the three streams. This is the essence of our being, our aliveness, which exists both in ourselves (soul) and above us in God. Therefore, while it could technically be called "passive unity of the spirit," it is better understood as unity of the essence or *essential unity*.

This is a realm where Christ our Helper is far more at home than we are. We have moved beyond matters of the world and flesh and are seeing the veil between heaven and earth beginning to part, if only slightly. However, as fascinating and awesome as this is, it might also be terrifying as we are completely out of our depth. Christ's supernatural adornment and divine help have been with us throughout this inward journey, of course, but at this point it becomes more like a stripping than an adorning. We are overwhelmed. We now have no choice but to abandon ourselves to the flood of God's grace in this essential unity and let Jesus take the oars. Daniel LaRusso lies helpless on the table with an injured leg, his life out of balance and his fight unfinished. Aladdin lies bound and dying at the bottom of the sea, unconscious and completely unable to save himself. Westley lies dead in the Pit of Despair after having his life sucked out by the Machine. If the helper does not step in, the journey is over and all is lost. The only hope is for a magic touch.

Reverend John describes our experience of essential unity as a divine "touch," which originates above activity and reason, though not *without* reason. Because our old "frenemy" Reason is now enlightened, it and our faculty of loving are able to perceive, to feel, this touch. We mustn't rely on Reason, but it does have its place. Again, the essence of our being is both *beyond* us and *within* us.

The woman who has suffered for twelve years with a chronic issue of blood is sure that her cure lies in Jesus's touch. This turns out to be true, and Jesus tells her, "Take heart, daughter, your faith has healed you" (Matt 9:22). This incident is bracketed by the story of a synagogue leader whose

2. John of Ruusbroec, *Spiritual Espousals*, b1271–73.

daughter has just died. He pleads with Jesus, "Come and put your hand on her and she will live" (v. 18). After pausing along the way to help the bleeding woman, Jesus comes to the little girl, takes her by the hand, and she gets up (v. 25). In both cases it is the divine touch of Jesus in cooperation with the desperate faith of the seeker that brings healing. While our ideal would be a real physical touch (imagine Jesus actually taking your hand in his!), the divine origin of the touch is just as real for us here and now as it was for these "daughters." The essence of our being *above* us in God meets the divine essence of life *within* us as we let go and turn in faith to Christ our Helper and Bridegroom.

This divine touch is the origin of all grace and gifts, and it is the last intermediary between God and us. Beyond this final go-between is the origin of the touch, the Trinity, dwelling in incomprehensible brightness in the still essence of being. It is from there that Christ as Bridegroom, by means of the touch, again draws us to "go out" to him. Here, in a subtle shift of metaphor, Reverend John has us plunging into the fountain, digging into the ground to reach the living vein of water, only to be blinded by the divine brightness of God's incomprehensible light. We dive into a well and end up in blindingly bright light. It makes no sense. But does it have to?

Our enlightened Reason is desperate to know the origin of the touch and to reach the depths of the fountain. But once again, even enlightened Reason can get in the way. We want to take hold of and control this essence of our being that is above us in God. And yet, as we previously encountered in the transition from the Active Life to the Inner Life, so here again is a threshold at which that fickle character, Reason, can go no farther. However, now we know how to cross the threshold. Only Mr. Miyagi can fix Daniel's leg. Only Genie can raise Aladdin from the bottom of the sea. Only Miracle Max can revive Westley from his state of being "mostly dead." And only Christ our Helper can bring us into our essential being in God. We must let go of control if we want to cross over into this deeper, essential realm, because "reason and intelligence fail in the face of the divine brightness and remain outside, before the door."[3] But once again, where Reason fails and must remain outside, blinded trusting love is allowed in. Will we give ourselves over and let ourselves be led inside? Christ the Bridegroom, the one who calls, can be answered now only by Christ the Helper, the one who leads with love.

---

3. John of Ruusbroec, *Spiritual Espousals*, b1308–9.

The Storm of Love

Love leads us in. It's a good thing, too, because Reason could never handle what is inside. We plunged into the fountain of God's grace and ended up in the blinding light of our essential being in God. We let Christ take our hand and lead us and now, in yet another surreal shift, we find ourselves in a bright room with a banquet prepared for us. Every dish imaginable is served . . . except the dish of satisfaction. Once again we experience *epektasis*, that eternal hunger that always fails to be satisfied. We taste the blissful honey of God's goodness, yet our experience is still limited by our struggling humanity. It is like attempting to contain an uncreated good in a created vessel, like trying to bottle love. We want desperately to eliminate anything that stands between us and God, even the means by which we experience God. We want to experience God *with God*. But we can't . . . not yet, anyway.

A storm begins to gather, rolling clouds and groaning thunder and flashes of lightning. It is the storm and strife of love, in which God's Spirit and our spirit are wounded the most by love as they flash and shine into each other, with God's touch and our craving becoming one overflowing love.[4] Remember that this is beyond intellect and rationalizing. This is a storm of blinding and wounding love. Such a profound encounter with God is bound to leave us creatures wounded. Just ask Jacob, who wrestled with God to the point not only of being wounded, but also of being re-named, becoming forever known as *Israel*, "he struggles with God" (Gen 32:22–32). It changes us. This is also part of our experience of salvation, another point at which our impairment and woundedness are met by, and united with, Christ's atoning woundedness and perfecting love. We cannot be the same after this.

It's all rather confounding. We were starting to be able to handle God's grace and love uniting with and transforming our body and mind—redirecting and reforming our appetites and senses, our awareness and understanding and will. But God's grace and love now transforming the essence of our very being knocks us for a loop. We're like Nicodemus, the respected teacher, when Jesus tells him about being born again from above (John 3:1–15). For Jesus it's a very basic concept, but Nicodemus, with all his learning and training, can only stammer, "How can this be?"

4. John of Ruusbroec, *Spiritual Espousals*, b1340–59.

Likewise, our present encounter with Christ as both Bridegroom and Helper occurs above our disciplines and lessons, which is why we have to let go and let ourselves wonder, "How can this be?" Our quests for the heart and the spirit took us as far as we could go before the divine undertow started ebbing back toward the fountain of God's grace and into the mysterious underground vein from which it all erupts. Our only options were to fight to stay in control, or to let Christ rescue us and carry us where we cannot go on our own.

Way-Stop #7: Reflection

This excursion is done. In some ways it was done before it began. On this strange quest for our essence via the Journey into the Fountain, God has touched us and blinded us, served us a blissful banquet and wounded us in the storm of love. We got there, into God's presence, but we never really took hold of our essence the way we were able to take hold of our heart and spirit, that is, our body and mind. It was all too confusing and overwhelming. Honestly, it was a quest that was doomed to fail.

We've encountered the challenge of Rainer Maria Rilke's words:

> Have patience with everything that remains unsolved in your heart. Try to love the questions themselves, like locked rooms and like books written in a foreign language. Do not now look for the answers. They cannot now be given to you, because you would not be able to live them. It is a question of experiencing everything. At present you need to live the questions. Perhaps you will gradually, without even noticing it, find yourself experiencing the answer, some distant day.[5]

Any frustration we might feel likely stems from a belief that we would finish this quest with answers. Instead, we probably now have more and bigger questions. The soul is like that. So we can imagine the labyrinth of questions to be found in the essence of our being as it is found in God.

The soul is elusive, even though it is part of us. This most essential part of our being is located both within us and beyond us, in God. The soul is much more like a river running through us than a pond inside us. It flows to us and from us with no well-marked boundaries. So we are limited in

---

5. Rilke, *Letters to Young Poet*, 35.

our ability to control it. This is why our sometime nemesis Reason can be so troublesome in our journey.

Even the part of our soul that is within us can only really be accessed and developed indirectly, by what is appropriately known as "indirection"— typically found in practices like silence, solitude, fasting, meditation, and the like. We can take heart that, by giving our all to the journey so far, we've been doing what we can for our soul. Additionally, the practice of worship can be especially helpful here (as always). Both corporately and alone, with psalms and hymns and spiritual songs, through God's revelation in Scripture and in the natural world, and in whatever brings us to God in devotion and adoration and delight—we do well to keep ourselves oriented in a Godward direction. After all, we become like what we worship.

Nevertheless, failure was actually the point in our Quest for the Essence. As Isaac of Nineveh (ca. 613–700) explains, the "delight of the mysteries of created things that are seen . . . is the first summit of knowledge"; but we must "confess incomprehensibility" and press on through the inner journey if we want "to find Him who is within you."[6] It turns out that our life is bigger than we'd thought. The only way to succeed in this quest was to "confess incomprehensibility" and abandon our efforts to God's grace. Having done so, we are still going. So we must press on. For somehow, despite the many ways the Bridegroom has come and we have gone out, we have yet "to meet him" on this Road through the Inner Life. But take heart . . . our treasure awaits!

Bearings

- ❖ *Location*: the Road > the Inner Life > "the bridegroom comes; go out" in the essence (soul)

- ❖ *Key Concepts*: God as flowing, ebbing sea; essential unity; the essence of our being within us (soul) and above us (in God); divine touch; storm of love; indirection

- ❖ *Practice*: worship

---

6. Isaac of Nineveh, *On Ascetical Life*, 4.55, 65, 66.

Part III

THE TREASURE

8

THE TREASURE OF BEING

BIFF: Why am I trying to become what I don't want to be? What am I doing in an office, making a contemptuous, begging fool of myself, when all I want is out there, waiting for me the minute I say I know who I am!...

WILLY, *with hatred, threateningly*: The door of your life is wide open!

BIFF: Pop! I'm a dime a dozen, and so are you!

WILLY, *turning on him now in an uncontrolled outburst*: I am not a dime a dozen! I am Willy Loman!

—Arthur Miller, *Death of a Salesman*

*I*S IT ALL WORTH *it?* It seems like a rather nonspecific question. But we know what it means, because each of us asks it in one way or another. For many, the answer turns out to be "no." We climb to the top of a ladder only to realize it was leaning against the wrong wall. We put in years of sacrifice and struggle. Perhaps we even attain the treasure we sought. But the treasure turns out to be anything but. It quickly loses its luster and we are left feeling empty and worthless, a dime a dozen. Maybe we look back at what we've sacrificed and realize we let go of some real treasures along the way. The thing we were striving for—possessions, position, power, profit— turns out not to fill the empty place inside us. Even the things most worthy of our efforts—family, country, equality, nature, peace, community, and the like—seem to drift in and out of our grasp, eluding our attempts to treasure them in a tangible way. In the end, the result of a lifetime of effort is out of our hands.

Is it all worth it? We answer that question with our answer to another question: What do I treasure? We might do just fine spending our life on a profitable career, a healthy family, serving a community and country, caring for creation, wielding positive influence, or any number of various marks of success. Many such things could be considered worthy uses of our time and talents, even of great value to us and to others. But if they hold the place as our life's greatest treasure, we are sure to find that place vacant in the end. So, our question might be answered in this way: *Yes, it's all worth it, but only if I recognize it as merely part of the journey to life's real treasure.* This is a key piece to the "more to life" and "more to myself" puzzle.

Luke Skywalker helped defeat the Empire, became a Jedi knight, and reconciled with his father; but none of these was his real treasure. Dorothy Gale traveled over the rainbow, met the Wizard of Oz face to face, and came to appreciate the value of home; but none of these was her real treasure. Bilbo and Frodo Baggins each left the Shire, possessed the coveted and powerful Ring, and helped save Middle Earth; but none of these was either's real treasure. And Elle Woods got into Harvard Law School, cracked a tough legal case, and fell in love with a good guy; but none of these was her real treasure.

For these heroes and for so many others—both fictional and real—the greatest treasure of their journey is the person they became along the way. The adventures and quests, the training and magical gifts, the victories, the relationships, all are of greatest value when they fit together to make a life. But what sort of life makes it all worth it?

The Treasure We Seek

One of Jesus's more troubling teachings gets at this question: "If anyone comes to me and does not hate father and mother, wife and children, brothers and sisters—yes, even their own life—such a person cannot be my disciple. And whoever does not carry their cross and follow me cannot be my disciple" (Luke 14:26–27). This is definitely not a passage typically featured on Christmas cards: "I hate my family. I hate myself. I hate you. Merry Christmas!" But despite its harsh tone, Jesus's honesty about the cost of discipleship is as loving as anything (and everything) else he ever taught.

He is not speaking here of competing religions (his audience was probably completely Jewish), though they can certainly be distractions. Instead, he is speaking of what we treasure, "for where your treasure is, there your heart will be also" (Matt 6:21). If we choose to say yes to the way of Christ, then there is no place for competing allegiances and intentions, no matter how seemingly noble. He does not allow it. The way of Christ, starting back with prevenient grace and then the school of the kingdom of the soul and so on, leads to union with God and the life God is living. That is our treasure, our North Star, our "one thing." That's the sort of life that is worth all the effort and trials of the journey. All else must emerge from that, and it will be much stronger and more meaningful for having done so.

To address the elephant in the verse, the word "hate" was likely hyperbole, which was a typical rabbinical teaching device that Jesus was rather fond of (as in "easier for a camel to go through the eye of a needle" and "remove the log from your own eye"). We might not get Jesus's humor as much today, but such things helped impress his teaching upon the minds of his hearers. So, "if you want to be my disciple you must hate your family and your own life" makes a pretty strong impression. Although it's also true that the sociopolitical context of intense persecution in which Jesus's followers would soon find themselves might have called for a little healthy hatred. Things like betrayal by family members and attachment to worldly possessions and the looming possibility of execution were all very legitimate threats to one's faith, requiring deep scrutiny and difficult prioritizing.

Either way, the truth remains for us today: no matter what supreme value we and/or others place on all our life projects—including something as noble as family—not one of them is worthy of being considered the greatest treasure. And honestly, it isn't really fair to those others (or to ourselves) to make them carry such a burden. The only thing that lasts, that transcends and yet impacts all the rest, and that not even death can separate us from, is our life with God. Recognizing and addressing everything—*everything*—as part of our journey to union with God is what makes it all worth it.

In his book *On Christian Teaching*, Augustine employs our familiar metaphor of a journey to clarify the nature of life's true treasure, which he does by distinguishing between enjoyment (Latin *frui*) and use (*uti*). We should imagine ourselves exiled in a foreign land, he says, knowing that we will find true happiness—enjoyment, fruitfulness, *frui*—only in our homeland. Home is our goal, our treasure. So we begin the journey home, employing different vessels and encountering various people and places and situations, all of which are of use (*uti*) for the journey. But we should not stop and settle for such things, abandoning the goal and treasure of home in exchange for something that was supposed to be of use only along the way. Useful and even enjoyable as some things might be, they are not the source of our true enjoyment and fruitfulness, which will be found only upon returning home to the embrace of God.

Augustine even goes so far as to say, "If we wish to return to our home country, where alone we can be truly happy, we have to use this world, not enjoy it."[1] It seems harsh, but he goes on to explain that we can love and enjoy things to the extent that they point us home to God. It's a matter of perspective and priorities, a matter of treasure. We should not "enjoy" the world in the sense of the things of the world becoming our goal. Whatever we love—the created world, our family and neighbors, our bodies and selves, our enemies—should be loved as a means to our journey to God. However, lest it sound like Augustine is advocating merely "using" people, he explains that through compassion and service we should also help others on their journey home to God. Real love is found only in such God-focused mutuality. In the end, Augustine says, we should love the journey itself because it leads us to the One who is Love.

In that spirit, as we established from the beginning, we are on a classic romantic quest to be united with our true Love.[2] That union is the treasure of our heroic journey, what Joseph Campbell calls the "ultimate boon" and Vladimir Propp calls the "object of search."[3] As with any treasure worthy of a quest, this treasure is multifaceted and life-changing. And that only becomes more the case when the sought-after treasure is union with the hero's true Love. So, with Reverend John's guidance we'll look in this section—The Treasure—at the four ways we experience this union. Some will be familiar, some altogether new, and each is higher and deeper and more profoundly life-altering than the previous.

1. Augustine of Hippo, *Doctr. chr.* 1.4.4.

2. Northrop Frye describes the romance as the completion of a quest with three main stages: "the stage of the perilous journey and the preliminary minor adventures; the crucial struggle, usually some kind of battle in which either the hero or his foe, or both, must die; and the exaltation of the hero." Frye, *Anatomy of Criticism*, 187. These stages are seen in Ruusbroec's Active, Inner, and Contemplative Lives, and perfected in his Common Life.

3. See Campbell, *Hero with Thousand Faces*, 148–63; and Propp, *Morphology of the Folktale*, 54.

Our Bare Being: Natural Unity Revisited

We are nearing the end of our long journey through our Inner Life, the second stage of our larger journey. We're approaching the last part of this stage's version of our mystical earworm: See, the bridegroom comes! Go out *to meet him*! However, it will still take us a little while to get there ("and miles to go before I sleep"). At this point, Reverend John sets the stage for our meeting with the Bridegroom in the Inner Life by offering a reminder about our own true nature.

Having taken hold of the supernatural adornment of the unity of our heart/bodily life and spirit/mental life, we were left reeling in the midst of our essential life—our fundamental being in God, which is manifested (at least in part) in our soul. We've torn back the coverings and are set to behold our true, naked selves, in order to begin to "be further clothed, so that what is mortal may be swallowed up by life" (2 Cor 5:4 NRSV). That's where Reverend John picks up the narrative here, with a closer examination of what we discussed previously as "the making of a hero."

Stripped down to our bare being, the core and essence of our life is constantly receiving the coming Christ, without intermediary and without cease. Christ is constantly coming to us in the depths of our being, with nothing between us. The essence and the life that we are in God, in our eternal Image, and which we have and are in ourselves according to our essential being (our soul), are all without intermediary and inseparable from God.

Basically, God is always actively present in the depths of our soul, and that unity does not require the supernatural adornment of grace because it exists directly in God. Therefore, "the spirit, according to its innermost, most sublime part, receives without cease the impress of its eternal image and of divine brightness in its bare nature."[4] We are a magic mirror, into which and through which God is always being imaged.

This is the natural unity of each human with God, which exists as *essential unity* (passive) in the essence of our bare being, in the *unity of the spirit/mind* (active), which is the domain of the higher faculties (memory, understanding, will), and in the *unity of the heart*, our bodily life. Reverend John cautions that this natural unity "makes us neither holy nor blessed, for all persons, good and evil, have this within themselves, but this is certainly

---

4. John of Ruusbroec, *Spiritual Espousals*, b1405–7.

the first cause of all holiness and all blessedness. And this is the meeting and the union between God and our spirit in our bare nature."[5]

So, God's image in the mirror of our life might be clear and faithful or cloudy and distorted—either we are like God because of grace and virtues, or we are unlike God because of sin. Yet either way, we are essentially and actively grounded in relationship to God, and with a divine light that shines through us and aids us in faithfully reflecting God, without which we cannot move on to higher states of union with God and our true self. In our natural state, then, all humans could be considered fundamentally made for the calling to this mystical-heroic journey we are presently on. Each of us has the spark of the soul. We are hardwired for this adventure. This truth about our bare being is of great value, though of itself it is not the treasure we seek.

Living into Our Essence

By now we should be coming to understand that if our ontology—our philosophy of being—were summarized in a word, the word would be "union." That is not only the "one thing" that we are after (in its higher states), but it is also the "one thing" that defines us. As humans we are fundamentally a three-part union within ourselves—heart, spirit, essence (body, mind, soul)—and are united with God naturally and, potentially, supernaturally. As Reverend John explained at the beginning of the inner journey, "We possess this unity in ourselves and, in fact, above ourselves, as a principle and support of our being and our life."[6] Possessing, or living into, this unity—both in ourselves and above ourselves—has been the driving force of this entire journey on the Road through the Inner Life. This is how we "go out" to the constant "coming" of Christ our Bridegroom. And this will continue to drive and inform our journey to our true treasure.

What we are trying to do here, before pressing on, is to stop ourselves from confusing the roles we play with the person we truly are. Again, many of the roles we fill are necessary, admirable, even noble. But they are not the essence of our true being. How many of us experience the existential crisis that results from this discovery at some point (often in midlife). We try to deal with it in various ways, many of them unhealthy, including merely exchanging one role for another, or reverting back to an earlier role in which

5. John of Ruusbroec, *Spiritual Espousals*, b1435–38.
6. John of Ruusbroec, *Spiritual Espousals*, b40–42.

we think we were happier and had more control. But if we continue confusing our roles with our true self, then we will continue pursuing or settling for treasures that are actually only markers (or distractions) on the map to the real treasure.

So, crisis or no, we do well to undertake the journey we're presently on, which includes allowing God to strip away our many layers—both good and bad—in order to lay us bare. At that point, in that condition, we will be able to see the truth of the classic Christian doctrine of creation: *esse qua esse bonum est* (being as being is good). This original blessedness is a truth that so many miss out on when it is replaced with a fixation on original sin. It's true of creation as a whole, and it's true of us individually: to be is good . . . very good (see Gen 1:31). There's the answer to Hamlet's desperate question.

Of course there is sin—actions and states of mind and attitudes of the will that are opposed to God and God's way. A pretty strong case could even be made that this is our dominant inclination. We (and creation itself) were and are in need of Christ as savior, God the Son showing the way and being the way to full participation in the life of God. But "sinner" is not our fundamental identity and should not define us. Not only was our life not an accident or unplanned (regardless of the circumstances of our birth), but we exist in dynamic union with God, a relationship that is manifested in all aspects of our being and is also held above our being in the divine embrace.

Way-Stop #8: Reflection

Why am I trying to become what I don't want to be? Biff Loman's desperate appeal to his even more tragically desperate father is perhaps the most clarifying question we can ask ourselves. It is a question that this entire quest for the true self is set on addressing. And nowhere is the issue more decisively confronted than in the growing experience of union with God, our love and boon and the object of our search.

Our present journey of recognizing and living more and more into this relationship of union is actually an expression of the fundamental goodness of our being. We are not trolls and hags disguising ourselves as princes and princesses. Just the opposite! By God's love and grace we are diamonds in the rough, heirs of God's kingdom with divinity in our spiritual DNA. Shouldn't our treasure and desires reflect this? As C. S. Lewis explains,

It would seem that Our Lord finds our desires not too strong, but too weak. We are half-hearted creatures, fooling about with drink and sex and ambition when infinite joy is offered us, like an ignorant child who wants to go on making mud pies in a slum because he cannot imagine what is meant by the offer of a holiday at the sea. We are far too easily pleased.[7]

But the truth lies deep down, in a cave or some underworld, representing the deepest—and often scariest—aspects of ourselves. Like Dorothy entering the Wicked Witch's castle, this is typically where the hero confronts his or her foe. But what exactly is the nature of this foe? During his Jedi training with Yoda in the swampy world of Dagobah, Luke Skywalker faces the cave, which contains, as Yoda explains, "Only what you take with you." In the darkness Luke finds Darth Vader, confronts him and cuts of his head, only to find his own face behind Vader's mask. So it is that the cave often reveals our true enemy to be ourselves.

Now, on the brink of uncovering our treasure, we must enter a dark realm to confront our false self and reveal our true self. Here, again, we do well to employ the joint practice of silence and solitude, and perhaps even a retreat by which we remove ourselves for a time from our day-to-day lives.

One of the difficulties of this practice, which is likely why it is so often avoided, is confronting the thoughts and feelings—and the false self—that plague us. We sit in silence and our minds are distracted by seemingly trivial thoughts, as well as haunted by mistakes and temptations and fears. However, like a pain in the body that helps us locate a problem for treatment, those thoughts and feelings are often the very things that are telling us where we need help, exposing masks we are wearing and false treasures we are hoarding in dark corners of our lives. Thus, keeping a journal in our solitude or attending a retreat guided by a spiritual director might be helpful.

We are rightly fearful of what we will find. It is troubling to confront our false self. And it can be shocking and unsettling to remove our masks and reveal our true self. But this is not because it is the horror we anticipated. On the contrary, we will be startled to find light streaming into this deep inner place. And even more startling, to the point of breaking our hearts with joy, we will find that God is there. We will begin to discover that our being is good—our bare being, with everything stripped away, is very good. Unlike our first parents, who realized that they were naked and

7. Lewis, *Weight of Glory*, 26.

became ashamed and hid from God (Gen 3:7–8), we can turn to God and throw our arms open and say, like Moses, "Here I am" (Exod 3:4). And to our eternal delight, we will find God already turned to us with open arms, saying, "Here I AM" (3:14). This has been God's posture all along.

Bearings

❖ *Location*: the Road (the Treasure) > the Inner Life > "See" (revisited)

❖ *Key Concepts*: union as treasure, ultimate boon, and object of search; enjoyment vs. use; Christ's constant coming and imaging; to be is good (original blessedness)

❖ *Practice*: silence and solitude; retreat

9

THE TREASURE OF BEING TRANSFORMED

Ships at a distance have every man's wish on board. For some they
come in with the tide. For others they sail forever on the horizon, never
out of sight, never landing until the Watcher turns his eyes away in
resignation, his dreams mocked to death by Time.

—Zora Neale Hurston, *Their Eyes Were Watching God*

I N *THE WIZARD OF OZ*, the Scarecrow had a brain the whole time. The
Tin Man had a heart. The Lion had courage. And Dorothy had the way
home on her feet (and in her heart) every step of the way. Oh, they were
given tangible symbols of their virtues—a diploma, a ticking heart clock, a
medal, ruby slippers. But the real treasure they sought was inside them—
was them—all along. Did they need the Wizard or Glinda to reveal this
to them? Perhaps. Did they need the journey in order to recognize and
live into this reality? Most certainly. Their true selves—seen in Scarecrow's
intelligence and Tin Man's compassion and Lion's courage and Dorothy's
homegrown nobility—eluded them until the nature of those true selves was
required for challenges and trials on the Road.

If we are coming to identify the *what* of our treasure as increasingly
intimate union with God, then our eyes should be starting to open to the
where of our treasure. Each *Wizard of Oz* character was sure their treasure was "out there," to be given by someone else or found at the end of a
rainbow. Truth be told, they did need an intermediary—a go-between—in
order to gain their treasure. But it wasn't a wizard or a good witch or access
to the inner sanctums of Emerald City they needed.

The only intermediary required was the yellow brick road, which is to say, the journey itself. The path to the treasure was through the companions and adversaries, the challenges and confrontations, the hopes and fears, and the inner and outer trials of the Road. Once the real treasure is discovered, however, it's goodbye, yellow brick road. There is no wooden chest or hallowed hall that contains it, no guardian to go through in order to access it. The treasure is within. It always has been. It always will be. It's who we are.

With that in mind, what is basically happening in these first two chapters of this section is something like retracing the steps of our journey (the third and fourth chapters will present something altogether new). It's the part of the story when a wise figure says something to the hero like "What you've been looking for has been with you the whole time," and then proceeds to explain how that is true. So here, we're looking back at how the treasure of union has been unfolding as we've walked the path of our adventure. We must take care, however, not to be complacent, for there are many new insights and opportunities for growth during this time of reflecting on the journey so far. In fact, now we have the benefit of hindsight, and the way Reverend John presents these familiar teachings is surprisingly fresh and potentially very fruitful. Not to mention the fact that what he is doing now is setting the stage for the most amazing things to come.

Super Union! with Intermediary: The Path of Grace and Virtues

"See, the bridegroom comes! Go out to meet him!" The treasure we seek is a life of complete union with God, articulated on our journey in the words "to meet him." John of Ruusbroec, acting as our Wizard, has revealed to us that this greatest of treasures has been inside us all along. Our very being is the result of, and is defined by, a relationship of natural union with God, without which we couldn't even exist. But there's much more. This natural union, which characterizes every human, can be supernaturally transformed. The image of God reflected in every human mirror can come to bear God's likeness so accurately and faithfully that it is as if there is no difference between the One reflected and the one doing the reflecting. Our precious treasure of union with God can become so real for us and in us that there is no longer any intermediary, any distance, and eventually any apparent difference between us.

"But how can this be?" we ask the Wizard of Ruusbroec.

"The grace of God is the path we should always travel," he replies, "if we are to enter into the simple being in which God gives Himself with all His richness, without intermediary."[1]

"Grace is a . . . path?" we ask, mentally scrambling to rework our understanding of grace.

"Yes," he says, "a path you've been walking for some time now."

"But I thought grace was just a thing God does, like a magic spell or something. So how is grace a path? And what do you mean by intermediary? And where are we . . . ?

"Let us keep going," he says, beginning to walk ahead, "and the answers will become clearer." He looks back at us and smiles. "Or perhaps the answers will become not so important."

Like a diamond with different facets, our treasure of union with God is experienced in four ways:

1. Natural Union

2. Supernatural Union *with* Intermediary

3. Supernatural Union *without* Intermediary

4. Union without Difference

Those first two are the journey we've already been on from the beginning, but Reverend John now talks about it all in terms of "intermediary," which is to say, a go-between or means to our union with God. He now uses this "intermediary" language to differentiate between the stages, demonstrating the nature and usefulness of an intermediary and highlighting how the need for an intermediary will ultimately be surpassed.

We have considered our Natural Union as that union that defines all humans. And we've been experiencing Supernatural Union—in the spirit of some hero stories we'll call it Super Union!—in the form of the quests for the supernatural adornment of that three-part Natural Union (heart/body, spirit/mind, essence/soul). These have characterized our journey to this point. Now that we have brought our supernaturally adorned senses and appetites, thoughts and feelings, and essential aliveness into the enterprise of discovering this treasure of divine union, we can continue the journey of actualizing—of taking hold of and owning and living from—that treasure.

---

1. John of Ruusbroec, *Spiritual Espousals*, b1493–95.

We are presently still in the stage of Super Union! *with* Intermediary, the second way of experiencing union with God. It's where we have spent the bulk of our journey. This stage itself is basically an intermediary—between stages—because it is a pathway of God's gracious activity that lies between the first way of experiencing union, Natural Union, and the third way, Super Union! *without* Intermediary (and ultimately the fourth way, Union without Difference). This is the journey that has been required in order for us to recognize and live into union as the reality of our life.

It takes a lot of work to unlearn the nature of reality and replace it with something altogether new, mysterious, and largely unseen! Before we can continue on to the even more startling facets of our treasure, the third and fourth ways of experiencing union, it behooves us to briefly reexamine and reframe some of the aspects of the journey so far. Reverend John has paused us here for a short review of some of the journey's mechanics and to let us get our bearings. After all, this present stage of the journey is the intermediary between our original Call and Departure and the upcoming fuller experiences of this treasure of divine union. And it is marked by the path of grace.

On this path of God's grace so far, our sin—which we can think of in terms of disunity with God and fragmentation within ourselves—has begun to be fully and deeply overcome, the ongoing way has been prepared, and our lives are becoming more and more fruitful. And this intermediary path goes both ways. Not only does "the bridegroom come" to us with transforming grace, but we also "go out" to him through the intermediary path of virtues, disciplines, and devotion. This back-and-forth energy generates the movement along this path, which is a road of constant renewal, with God giving new gifts and us always turning inward in a meeting of receptivity and growing into a higher life.

Reverend John describes this back-and-forth movement as an "active meeting" with the Bridegroom, experienced entirely through the intermediary of "the gifts of God and our virtues and the activity of our spirit," and he further notes that "without the mediation of the grace of God and of a loving, free conversion [i.e., transformation], no creature will be saved."[2] This, then, is the two-way path of salvation: grace and virtues. Being "saved" should never be considered in terms of a one-time and one-way transaction, but always as an ongoing process of cooperation with God's grace. We are not saved *by* our virtuous works, but we are saved by God's grace

2. John of Ruusbroec, *Spiritual Espousals*, b1513–17.

through our faith and *for* good works (Eph 2:8–10). What we are saved *from* is our separation from God and all the inner and outer fragmentation that results from that, which of course is what our journey is about. And who doesn't love a good redemption story?

High Life and Higher Love: The Gifts of the Holy Spirit

The path of grace and virtues that we've been traveling now begins to ascend. The dynamic between Christ the Bridegroom's coming to us (via grace and gifts) and our going out to him (via virtues and spiritual practices) continues to generate movement toward higher experiences and expressions of unity. God gazes on us as God's own dwelling place by way of our unity with him and our likeness to him. More and more we are bearing the family resemblance of God. God's will is to ceaselessly visit our God-unity by constantly being born anew in us, and to visit our Godlikeness by bestowing new gifts upon us so we can become ever more Godlike and radiant in virtues.

And that, in fact, is our response: becoming more and more like God and living a virtuous, Christlike life. All of this is really just a closer look at the supernatural adornment of our Natural Unity that we discussed previously. It's part of how Christ our Helper makes us over (the divine "bibbidi-bobbidi-boo"). Reverend John explains, "For in each new now, God is born in us. And out of this sublime birth, the Holy Spirit flows with all His gifts. Now, we should meet the gifts of God with likeness, and the sublime birth with unity."[3] So, God ceaselessly comes and shapes us to live more fully united with God and more like God, and we in turn keep going out to meet God for a fuller experience of unity and more faithful likeness. "In each new now, God is born in us" (that's too good not to repeat, and it puts a whole new spin on Christmas!). With this, we have a sign pointing the way to the higher life via the gifts of the Holy Spirit.[4]

The gifts of the Holy Spirit form the path to the higher experiences of union. But first, there's a caution sign: "God Alone" it reads. In order

3. John of Ruusbroec, *Spiritual Espousals*, b1528–30.

4. Ruusbroec does not use the term "gifts of the Holy Spirit," but his schema here is referencing a classic formulation developed by early church fathers to describe dispositions of the soul resulting from the Holy Spirit's action. The "gifts" are based on Isa 11:2–3, and should not be confused with the "fruit of the Spirit" of Gal 5:22–23, gifts of the Spirit mentioned in 1 Cor 12:7–10, and so on, though these are all important aspects of the true self that is addressed in this volume.

to walk the path to the higher life, we must have a singleness of focus that intends nothing but God alone. We must gather what we've learned so far and focus it all on God, resisting distractions and temptations to turn aside or back. This single intention that focuses solely on the likeness and unity of God is "the inward, enlightened, loving inclination of the spirit. *It is the foundation of all spiritual life*."[5] Our one thing. Our North Star. Our treasure. We must want God and only God, not even holy status or spiritual experiences. We must trust that everything we seek, including our true self, will be found in God alone.

Now, focused and fired up with God-intention, we can proceed along the upward path of the seven gifts of the Holy Spirit. The gifts are progressive, with each leading to the next, and Reverend John offers a reminder at each point about how they contribute to our God-unity and Godlikeness and are spurred on by our God-intention—all clearly vital concepts for moving along this path. Also, while there is much we can do to be more or less receptive and cooperative, it should be remembered that these are gifts bestowed by God the Holy Spirit, not superficial religious masks we can put on.

The first gift is *the fear of God*, demonstrated in part through obedience and submission to the teaching and authority of Scripture, the church, and the commandments of God. Some might bristle at such accountability, especially on this mystical path where we might think we're above such things. But nothing could be further from the truth. It is precisely along such lofty spiritual heights that we require the guardrails of revelation and tradition and trusted community. Also, many have come to associate the fear of God with something akin to awe rather than actual feelings of fear. And yet, while the description of awe is accurate, it should be born of a grave consideration of God's power and supreme authority. As Mr. Beaver said of Aslan, he isn't safe but he is good.

This gift is characterized by a willingness and readiness to do all good things for the sole purpose of pleasing God. The result of the fear of God is the conformity of our will to God's will, key to living the life God is living. Jesus was not above such humility before God, saying, "Not as I will, Father, but as you will" (Matt 26:39). And more than merely saying it, Jesus clearly lived it. Now, with the fear of God, we move on.

The second gift is *mercifulness*, which includes meekness and a generosity of heart. Meekness should of course not be mistakenly thought of

5. John of Ruusbroec, *Spiritual Espousals*, b1547–48 (emphasis added).

(as it often is) as mousiness or weakness. Instead, it should look like Christ as he reserved his power and authority and humbly gave himself to and for others, loving even his enemies.

Such a spirit of generous mercy and kindness results in our being more full of life and more like Jesus, who used the Parable of the Good Samaritan to illustrate neighborly mercy (Luke 10:29–37). For Jesus's Jewish hearers, the idea of a "good Samaritan" was a contradiction in terms. Yet because he was the one who showed mercy to the battered Jew, that despised outsider became the hero of Jesus's startling story. "Go and do likewise," Jesus concludes. Mercy results in resting more in God rather than seeking to assert more and more of our own power. So, with mercy, we continue.

The third gift is *knowledge*, which includes discernment and reasonableness, knowing what must be done or omitted and when to give or take. This knowledge is employed in making us more like the Holy Trinity—humble and obedient in light of the Father, reasonable and discerning in light of the Son, and generous and merciful in light of the Holy Spirit. We recall our earlier contemplation of the divine Persons as we sailed along the Stream of Understanding.

We should take care that this knowledge is not used for superficial religiosity but in order to consider and move toward the higher life of actual Trinity-likeness. Our appetite for knowledge about God and all God has made should be insatiable. Those on the journey of divine union should be the most curious people around, relentless in our pursuit of knowledge. This is the fullness of apprenticeship to Christ and his teaching, by which "you will know the truth, and the truth will make you free" (John 8:32). With knowledge, we move on higher.

The fourth gift of the Holy Spirit is *fortitude*, which is courage and inner strength in the face of challenges. This enables us to overcome prosperity and misfortune, profit and loss, hope and cares about earthly things, and all sorts of obstacles and divided attention and misplaced loyalties. We are usually quick to recognize the challenges of discomfort and need, but often less aware of the challenges of comfort and ease. Fortitude is a gift of discipline and self-mastery. We should take care to move beyond activities and signs, and on to the One to whom they lead, to nothing less than standing before the throne of the Holy Trinity. In this way we serve at God's table with thanks and praise and inner worship, drinking of the wine and tasting the crumbs that fall from the table.

THE TREASURE OF BEING TRANSFORMED

With this fortitude we are willing to pass beyond all gifts and consolations in order to find the One we love and, thus, to transcend all created things and master ourselves as powerful and free. We think of Jesus resisting the temptations of everything from bodily needs, to worldly power, to even the heights of religious achievement, all for the sake of complete devotion to God alone (Luke 4:1–13). So, with fortitude, we press on higher still.

The fifth gift of the Spirit is *counsel.* This is a particularly tough one, indicative of higher levels of spiritual maturity. It is characterized by satisfying the will and the counsel of God in both working and suffering, in self-forsakenness and in humble obedience. This gift is complicated and trying, in keeping with the blessings and trials of the Road. We move between experiences of elation and fiery love to something like a dark desolation. Reverend John explains, "At times God transfers us from His right hand side to the left, from heaven into hell, from all bliss into great misery, and it appears as though we were forsaken and disdained by God and by all creatures."[6] We can see exactly this in the life of Jesus, and it should not be thought of as punishment but as participation in God's life and love and mission. Having become familiar with John of the Cross's "dark night," we are now better able to recognize what is happening and to meet this challenge and receive this gift.

The gift of counsel is lived out primarily through renouncing our own agendas and submitting to what God is doing, succinctly and powerfully articulated by Jesus in his exemplary prayer: "Your kingdom come [not mine], your will be done [not mine]" (Matt 6:10). The words are familiar, but the reality can be trying. And yet, ideally God's kingdom is coming from within us and God's will and our will are becoming one and the same. With the gift of counsel, we continue.

The sixth gift of the Spirit is *understanding.* Just as the gift of counsel recalls the trials of the Road, so this gift of understanding reminds us of how prior stages are never left behind as we progress. We think of the sun filling the air with simple brightness, enlightening all forms and colors, and offering its power and warmth for the use and fruitfulness of others, all recalling our quest for the heart. And we remember the streams, which were said to establish our spirit in unity, to reveal the truth, and to forge a bond of love. So, likewise, this gift of understanding yields very similar effects: enlightenment and mastery in bodily life, simplicity in the memory, clarity in the understanding, and universal love in the will.

6. John of Ruusbroec, *Spiritual Espousals,* b1663–65.

The more we live out these characteristics, the more united and God-like we are becoming. This gift of understanding enables us to be what Jesus called "salt" and "light," bringing out the God-flavors and God-colors in the world (see Matt 5:13–16 MSG). So now, with understanding, we move on to the highest gift.

The seventh gift of the Spirit, *wisdom*, is actually the first gift God produces in us, but the last to be recognized. We've been using wisdom to perceive the other gifts, but we're only now able to realize it for the gift it is. As the gift of understanding reminded us of the Journey of the Sun (unity of the heart/body) and the Journey of the Streams (unity of the spirit/mind), this gift of wisdom recalls the Journey into the Fountain (unity of the essence/soul and life in God). This wisdom is experienced as a divine stirring or touch in the essence of our being. It erupts into grace and gifts and virtues. This divine stirring of the gift of wisdom is the innermost intermediary between God and us, between rest and activity, between time and eternity.

Once again, Reason's attempt to comprehend and explain this stirring and touch is met with failure, yet Reason is essential to recognize the presence of God's touch. It's like trying to follow the sun's rays to their source, which inevitably results in a futile attempt to peer into the sun. But still, by the sun we are able to see everything else. This is the way of the gift of wisdom. God's incomprehensible light cannot be experienced here without the intermediaries of God's grace and gifts. We rely on God to touch us anew every moment, so that at every moment we may be newer and more Godlike in virtues. If we will allow ourselves to be grounded in this deep life of God, we become the wise person who builds their house on the rock (Matt 7:24–27). This gift of wisdom integrates all the gifts into an immovable foundation in the essence of our being.

Way-Stop #9: Reflection

We can now look back and see the long road of Super Union! with Intermediary stretching and winding behind us. Christ our Helper has worked with the Holy Spirit to bless us and adorn us with gifts to produce greater Godlikeness and God-unity within us. Thanks to the seven gifts of the Holy Spirit, we have followed the path and reached a new height. This path—marked by the dynamic experience of Christ coming to us with grace and gifts and our going out to him with virtues and spiritual practices—has reached its culmination. It has led us *from* Natural Union and *to* the state of union that comes next: Super Union! *without* Intermediary. We now stand ready to encounter the One behind the light, behind the touch, and behind the grace.

Once again, if we are to go on, we must let go. As was the case previously, when we stripped away the coverings and dove down into the deep fountain of God's grace and light and feast of goodness, so again here we have reached our limit. All we can do now is abandon ourselves to God . . . again (and again and again). The process of unknowing and coming to rest in God continues. We are probably realizing that God and Christ are not exactly who or what we thought they were. Our cultural priorities and the things we thought were most important are perhaps not the treasure we thought they were. And we are not who we thought we were.

Ideally we are learning to let go of some of our inadequate ideas and misdirected goals and false narratives about God and life and ourselves. It can all be very refreshing. But it can also be disorienting. We must take care not to rush into another ramshackle belief system or start hastily pounding together a substitute spirituality. The wide-open spaces can leave us feeling exposed and insecure when we are used to narrow streets lined with cavernous man-made structures. But if we will let things be, we will find ourselves stretching out and growing into the larger space around us, which is to say, within us.

As we experience things like stripping away aspects of our false self and exposing and encountering our true self, a helpful practice would be some form of spiritual companioning. This might include meeting regularly with a spiritual director or a professional counselor or therapist. Or it might be what the Celtic Christian tradition calls a "soul friend," a relationship for mutual accountability, encouragement, and spiritual sharpening. The Methodist tradition promotes similar relationships in what were originally called "bands"—three or four people of the same gender who meet together regularly for honest accountability and support.

Our experience at this point might be likened to walking a long mountain road, with Christ at the top. We catch glimpses of him running back down and signaling to us, so we pick up the pace and run toward him. Then he turns around and runs on ahead to the higher life with the divine Unity and Trinity that awaits us. He disappears around the mountain, and we're left continuing on our own (or so it seems). Then we see him coming back to us again, so we run ahead, excited that we're making progress. But then he seems to be gone again. And so it goes, up and around, until we get to where we are now.

And yet, from some eternally deep and hidden place, a call still comes.

Bearings

◈ *Location*: the Road (the Treasure) > the Inner Life > "the bridegroom comes; go out" (revisited)

◈ *Key Concepts*: Supernatural Union with Intermediary; the path of grace and virtues; Godlikeness, God-unity, and God-intention; the seven gifts of the Holy Spirit (fear of God, mercifulness, knowledge, fortitude, counsel, understanding, wisdom)

◈ *Practice*: spiritual companioning

10

The Treasure of Being One

Gatsby believed in the green light, the orgiastic future that year by year recedes before us. It eluded us then, but that's no matter—tomorrow we will run faster, stretch out our arms farther.... And one fine morning—

—F. Scott Fitzgerald, *The Great Gatsby*

M ust the treasure forever remain at arm's length? Even the treasure we've found, a treasure worthy of the name and worthy of our lives, must at some point be able to be possessed. Will Scarecrow, Tin Man, Lion, and Dorothy forever require continuing journeys along endless yellow brick roads in order to access the true selves that have been revealed during their adventure? Or will they—and we—finally come to inhabit the journey's true treasure of transformation? Certainly we will always face life's everyday struggles and occasional crises that require the gifts and treasure of our *mediated* unity with God in its various facets. But our ideal is not to have to rely on the journey—the path of God's grace and our virtues—as a go-between. Though we never "arrive" in the sense of an end to our formative journey with God, surely we arrive at *something* in the sense of a transformation of our experience of unity with God and likeness to God.

In our corkscrew trip up the mountain of union, we have come around to see again where we previously followed the cycles of the sun and then followed along the three streams, though now we are surveying those stretches of the Road from a higher point of view. We have been led along the transformational upward path of the seven gifts of the Holy Spirit, and now we come around again to reconsider the fountainhead of the streams, that underground well of the essence of our being in God. We've experienced the startling revelations that the natural essence of our being is unity with God, and that God is supernaturally transforming that natural unity into something more and more like God. That process of transformation is what Reverend John finally came to call Supernatural Union with Intermediary, the intermediary being the back-and-forth relationship of God's grace and gifts working with our virtues and spiritual practices.

Now we are prepared for the even more startling experience of that essential union *without* the go-between of God's grace and our virtues. Instead of requiring the "bibbidi-bobbidi-boo" of Christ's supernatural adornment of our natural unity (though that is ongoing), we are ready to strip off everything and fall into the bare essence of our being in the divine embrace. Christ our Helper, with the gifts of the Holy Spirit, has now brought us to the penultimate stage of unity: Supernatural Union *without* Intermediary. Our head is again filled with our mystical earworm: See, the bridegroom comes! Go out to meet him! We are finally ready "to meet him," to unite with our beloved Bridegroom on the long Road of the Inner Life.

But first, a word of encouragement: We might be finding ourselves thinking, "Again with the 'essence' and 'meeting' stuff? I'm not sure I get it. It's pretty mysterious and confusing. Maybe just tell me what to *do* about all this." If that is the gist of our thinking, then we are illustrating two points. First, completely changing our understanding about the fundamental nature of reality takes time. The same way God has to tell us over and over to love each other because it just seems so hard to get, so the truth and the ramifications of our life's essence as deeply and inextricably united with God bears some repeating. And second, our constant inclination to *do* rather than simply to *be* is a subtle reminder that we are not quite getting it. When we talk about our essence, we are talking about our being. It is surprising how much work it takes just to let ourselves be, and for that to be enough. So for now, let's keep being . . . and let's keep going.

Super Union! without Intermediary: From Deep to Deep

As we've just looked more closely at God's supernatural adornment of our natural union, now we move on to reexamine what we find in the inner recesses where we encounter our essential being, the bare essence of our true self. We followed the sun and, with God's grace and our virtues, we stripped away the misguided desires of the heart/body. We followed the streams and, with God's grace and our virtues, we washed away the confusing dictates of the spirit/mind. We dug into the fountain of God's grace and the source of virtue and found the incomprehensible light of God's direct presence in our essence/soul. We were laid bare and powerless, overcome and wounded by God's love. Reverend John said that what lay beyond that experience was direct, unmediated union with the divine Trinity. And that is the holy ground on which we now stand.

This is where we finally "meet him." Here, the incomprehensible light of the divine Tri-Unity blinds and penetrates and transforms us. This is the deep inner calling in which, says Reverend John, "the abyss of God calls the abyss inward," as in the words of the psalmist: "Deep calls to deep in the roar of your waterfalls; all your waves and breakers have swept over me" (Ps 42:7).[1]

God's deep calls to our deep. The brightness of God's presence in our essential being blinds us in its dazzling incomprehensibility. It surrounds us in an embrace of fathomless love, overwhelming us and causing us to lose ourselves as we swim in "the wild darkness of the Godhead," which is to say the deep mystery of the Unity of Father, Son, and Spirit.[2] It is "wild darkness" because it is untamed and incomprehensibly bright and requires unknowing, abandoning ourselves to God, if we are to answer this call to the meeting of deep with deep.

This union with the Holy Trinity in its unfathomable Unity is only the result of the eternally intimate presence of God, and all we can do here is just *be*. This is new territory: Super Union! without Intermediary. It is characterized in three ways (because of course it is). Each characteristic works with the others, as all are describing the same state of union. We must watch our step, however, for each characteristic also has a potential pitfall, a deviation that will draw us more into ourselves and our natural state of union and less into supernatural union with God. In so doing, it draws us away from our true self rather than toward it.

Again, we should bear in mind that this is supernatural union, not natural, and that it is without intermediary, no longer reliant on the means or go-between of God's grace and our virtues. Though these forever continue as aspects of our life with God, we are moving on to a higher, more passive, and more profound experience of our treasure of divine union. In short, this is the direct experience of God, and it is God who is causing it.

1. John of Ruusbroec, *Spiritual Espousals*, b1867.
2. John of Ruusbroec, *Spiritual Espousals*, b1871.

Characteristic One: Emptiness vs. False Emptiness

So here we are in the wide-open space of our bare essential being. No strengths or accomplishments or activities to hide behind. We consider the first characteristic of our experience of Super Union! without Intermediary: *emptiness*. As a result of God's overwhelming light, we recognize darkness, bareness, and nothingness within. Our reliance on God alone to work continues as the failure of our activity is overcome by the activity of God's fathomless love. This is why we must learn simply to be, so that we can let God work. However, our continued will and inclination toward God results in a victory as we, in a sense, overcome God in an act of union between our spirit and God's Spirit. We're like a child tackling her parent in a joyous embrace. This is carefree abandon. Our spiritual strivings cease and we simply exist with God.

This union empties us of all activity and self-mastery, and it even has the potential somatic effect of rendering us immobile. Here we can see at work the anthropology and ontology we've explored: this state of possessing God is experienced in our essential being in God, flows forth into the unity of the spirit and higher faculties (memory, understanding, and will), and finally flows into our heart and bodily faculties, potentially resulting in immobility. The experience is something like a healthy numbness of soul and body, accompanied by an unusual clarity, as well as a feeling of well-being and a joy of living. It is a vast and holy and vulnerable emptiness.

The deviation from this manner of emptiness is *false emptiness*. It is something of a shadow mode and natural experience of emptiness, rather than the supernatural experience of true emptiness. We experience the goodness of being, but it is not the goodness of being with God. All people can experience a form of this emptiness and rest, and it is not sinful since it is part of our natural union with God. However, it is a deviation, even if only a slight one, that can eventually lead us far off course. It is part of what is only an imitation of the true treasure of complete union that we have sought to possess and to live into. We might recall Augustine's designation of use vs. enjoyment.

The key difference between emptiness and false emptiness, then, is our inclination toward God and God's loving presence transforming our being, as opposed to emptiness for its own sake—empty emptiness, we might say. We can think of a doting parent and child or a long-married couple content to sit and be "alone together," as opposed to a loner who forms his identity around his aloneness. False emptiness is associated with our false self, which seeks Godlikeness without God. With maturity we come to recognize the difference, and we are not satisfied with the unadorned, graceless rest and emptiness. Our questing nature impels us onward to eternal, God-oriented emptiness and the higher forms of union that still lie ahead. So we must guard against the deception of false emptiness by remaining lovingly inclined toward God in the rest of true emptiness, the peace of being.

Characteristic Two: Active Desire vs. Active Self-Seeking

The second characteristic of our experience of Super Union! without Intermediary is *active desire*. It is an inward perception or feeling in the ground of our own being in God, where all virtues end and begin, where we offer all virtues to God in worshipful desire, and where love lives within us. It is the vast space in the essence of our being that is reserved for God alone as our "one thing," our treasure. This second manner of experiencing unmediated Super Union! is actually the cause of the first, emptiness. We must first desire and love God if we are to enter the emptiness and rest with God above our activity. Thus, this active desire is intertwined with emptiness, because God's grace and our active love must both precede and follow emptiness and rest in God. We must *treasure* God in order for God to *be* our treasure.

Yearning love is a characteristic of this active desire, and it is yet another experience of *epektasis*, in which the hunger and thirst of love become so great that we must surrender ourselves every moment and fail in our activity, exhausting ourselves and becoming annihilated in love. We are hungry and thirsty for God, and there is always something more and something new to taste. Such annihilation is necessary for our constant renewal and movement toward deeper union, as living, we die; and dying, we come to live again.

We follow the lead of John the Baptizer and his affirmation, "He must increase, but I must decrease" (John 3:30 NRSV), taking hold of Jesus's promise that "whoever loses their life for me will find it" (Matt 16:25). This must not simply be a nice idea that is more romantic than practical. No, it is the very core of self-sacrificing love for the God who, in Christ, is the embodiment of such love. It is the connection of mutual vulnerability. This constant pursuit of God and renewal in God characterizes our second way of experiencing Super Union! without Intermediary, active desire.

The deviation from active desire leads to the path of *active self-seeking*. This results from splitting the close relationship between emptiness and active desire. It occurs when we try to cultivate rest in emptiness without the inner desire for and devotion to God. We turn away from God and back toward ourselves and our natural state of union, desiring and seeking pleasure and rest for their own sakes, rather than as an aspect of unmediated union with God. This is often seen in pop mysticism and superficial spirituality.

The difference is largely in the will, the inclination toward self rather than God, though the appearance and even some of the experiences of God-seeking desire and its deviation of self-seeking are similar. Reverend John says (and we know he's right) that some people who are still attached to self do great works for fame and popularity, for a reputation as pious and holy. They might even achieve such a reputation, becoming known as very "spiritual" and even writing best-selling books and filling churches or auditoriums and gaining a large following. They seek reward, for all natural love favors itself. Once again, this self-seeking is a characteristic of the false self, as opposed to desiring the God in whom the true self is found.

So, again, the difference is largely intention, marked by either the supernatural adornment of God's grace or merely moving according to one's natural love. Reverend John explains, "For charity is a love-bond which carries us away and in which we renounce ourselves and are united with God and God with us. But natural love turns back upon itself and upon its ease, and always remains alone."[3] Thus, as the seemingly contradictory experiences of emptiness and active desire form a dialectical interplay that generates movement into God, so the deviations of false emptiness and active self-seeking work dialectically to move us into our natural self and away from the treasure of true divine union.

Characteristic Three: Inner Righteousness vs. Inner Unrighteousness

The third characteristic of our experience of Super Union! without Intermediary is *inner righteousness*, which is to say a right and just and transformative relationship with God. This third characteristic of unmediated union is a synthesis of the other two: emptiness (rest) and desire (work). Those two seem like opposites but, as we've seen, they actually fortify each other in a non-dualistic cooperation.

The result of the interplay of emptiness and active desire—of rest and work—is a new relationship of ceaseless mutuality, of dynamic union

3. John of Ruusbroec, *Spiritual Espousals*, b2048–50.

between God and us. This dynamic union is inner righteousness, and it makes the union of us in God, and God in us, whole and undivided. We are wholly in God, where we rest in joy. And we are wholly within ourselves, where we love God with our works. And God calls us and guides us every moment to fresh rest and activity.

We are constantly beckoned by God and held in God's gaze, leading to a renewal in our practice of virtues and in the deep joy of resting in God. This, says Reverend John, is a true spiritual life, a life of consolation, peace, joy, beauty, and true riches, and a life that will abide eternally and only move to a higher state after our earthly life is done. We are hungry and thirsty, for we see the angels' food and heavenly drink. We labor greatly in love, for we see our rest. We are pilgrims, for we see our homeland. We struggle in love for victory, for we see our crown.[4] If we will live into this treasure, we will show ourselves becoming the true heroes we are made to be.

An image of these three characteristics of Super Union! without Intermediary is the powerful fifteenth-century icon *The Trinity*, by Andrei Rublev. In the icon we see the divine Persons sitting together in a circular composition, with the Son and the Spirit inclining their heads toward the Father, who faces them and gently returns their inclination. Part of the brilliance of the icon is that the Trinitarian circle opens toward us, inviting us to enter the image and, so, to enter the company of the Trinity. Here we simply inhabit the space that opens to us (emptiness), leaning in and inclining ourselves toward the divine Persons (active desire), and existing in time and space and eternity as part of the divine circle (inner righteousness).

However, there is another way: *inner unrighteousness.* This potential deviation from righteousness, the unrighteous life, is essentially a life of being a contemplative with nothing to contemplate. Like the true life of righteousness, this unrighteousness is the result of a synthesis, in this case a synthesis of the deviations of false emptiness and active self-seeking, basically simultaneous rest and work apart from God's company. Those following this path have settled for their unadorned natural state, dedicated to self-help and self-righteousness, as opposed to selfless love and devotion to God as revealed apart from their own conceptions of the divine. This would be Rublev's icon with the Trinity removed. Only the observer remains, inhabiting the empty space and a circle unto him- or herself. Tragically, this is exactly what many consider the goal of the mystic way.

4. See John of Ruusbroec, *Spiritual Espousals*, b1949–56.

Such people consider themselves so free and united with their own idea of God that they have no more use for the church, for God's commandments, for divine law, or for holiness of heart and life. They consider themselves above such things, and their claims of freedom lead them to do whatever their natural self desires. They claim to be justified in both godly and ungodly behavior, often maintaining that it all comes from the Holy Spirit. They live on the basis of self-justification, as opposed to the divine assurance of true righteousness. Essentially, those who deviate onto this path become their own gods for themselves. A dangerous path indeed!

In contrast to all of these misguided deviations, we must always look to Christ as the model of the perfect Inner Life. We see this throughout the Gospels, especially in Christ's proclamations such as "My food is to do the will of him who sent me and to finish his work" (John 4:34); "Let anyone who is thirsty come to me and drink . . . rivers of living water will flow from within them" (7:37–38); "Believe me when I say that I am in the Father and the Father is in me; or at least believe on the evidence of the works themselves" (14:11); and so on. Jesus lived and exemplified perfect, unmediated union with God—true emptiness and rest, true desire and work, and true righteousness and right relationship—in each and all parts of his being.

And, miracle of miracles, Christ our Helper promises us, "Very truly I tell you, whoever believes in me will do the works I have been doing" (John 14:12). We might think of this as literally meaning we will be able (and called) to do the same works—perhaps including miracles—that Jesus did. But the context indicates that Jesus is promising something much bigger: we will be able to live in the same divine mutuality (the Father in me and I in the Father) that he enjoys. The works and miracles, then, are merely expressions of that relationship. We should pause and consider this for a moment: we are invited by the truest embodiment of perfect divine-human union to follow and share in that same union. And not only invited, but we are promised that walking in the way of Christ *will* lead us to a life of such union, with all that means. This is everything. And this is what it is "to meet him" at the end of the long Road through the Inner Life.

Way-Stop #10: Reflection

Wake the children and call the neighbors! We have finally reached the end of our journey through the Inner Life. Let celebrations abound! And what a long, strange trip it's been. We have gone on quests through our heart/body, through our spirit/mind, and through our essence/soul. And by revisiting those quests we are finally beginning to fully get hold of our treasure of the more (though not yet the most) profound and intimate experiences of union with God: Super Union! We are still on the Road, but we have come through the Inner Life and are as prepared as we can be for what comes next.

We have looked back on our adventures and seen how we've had our treasure within us all along, but the journey was necessary for us to truly recognize and embrace it. And then, beyond possessing the treasure, we are finally coming to be possessed and transformed by it, to more fully live into our true selves as united with God in the essence of our very being, both within ourselves and above ourselves in God. Now we rest and worship and love in the bright, unfathomable embrace of the divine Unity and Trinity.

And speaking of rest, that is probably a helpful practice to engage (by disengaging) at this point. Rest is good, practiced and commanded by God (see Gen 2:2; Exod 20:8–10). Keeping a weekly Sabbath day is an ideal, in which we refrain from work and hyper-connectivity, and focus instead on rest and worship and family and the like. Other ways of practicing rest can include a daily siesta for unplugging and maybe napping, a monthly or quarterly day or weekend of retreat, a yearly extended vacation, and so on. The point is to program regular rhythms of rest into our busy lives so we remember and experience the "more to life" and "more to ourselves" and "worthy treasure" we've been discovering. We are human *beings*, after all, not human *doings*.

The teachings of this chapter and the practice of rest might be difficult for us. We live in a pull-yourself-up-by-your-bootstraps culture, in which many of us are made to feel guilty for taking time for rest and self-care. Our coaches told us to rub some dirt on our injuries and get back in the game. We might have been inclined (or instructed) to take a relentless and often self-destructive work ethic into our spiritual lives. Perhaps this has resulted in a line of thinking that says we can impress and even manipulate God with how religious and disciplined we are and, on the flip side, that God is disappointed and angry with our failures, perhaps punishing us as a result. So we try harder . . . or we give up.

For some, such harsh judgment and self-criticism might have given way to understandable resentment toward the religious systems—and even toward the God—associated with the destructiveness. We might have abandoned the whole enterprise. Or perhaps we now find ourselves stumbling through the pitfalls mentioned in this chapter, avoiding the God we've come to associate with destructive religiosity while still trying to retain a version of mystical spirituality.

Wherever we find ourselves, may we treat ourselves with the grace and mercy we would hope to receive from a good and loving God. Furthermore, hopefully this journey is helping us to see: yes, a harsh and judgmental and demanding God needs to be abandoned; because no, that is not the God revealed in Jesus of Nazareth. While there is profound power and beauty in the Christian religion, Christianity is not Christ. The idea that if our experience of Christianity has been disappointing or damaging we must therefore abandon the way of Christ is a tragically false dilemma.

May God save us from allowing broken institutions and flawed leaders to keep us from our treasure, from entering the Trinitarian circle that opens toward us, wherein lies the fulfillment of Christ's invitation: "Are you tired? Worn out? Burned out on religion? Come to me. Get away with me and you'll recover your life. I'll show you how to take a real rest. Walk with me and work with me—watch how I do it. Learn the unforced rhythms of grace. I won't lay anything heavy or ill-fitting on you. Keep company with me and you'll learn to live freely and lightly" (Matt 11:28–30 MSG).

Bearings

- *Location*: the Road (the Treasure) > the Inner Life > "to meet him"
- *Key Concepts*: Supernatural Union without Intermediary; emptiness vs. false emptiness; active desire vs. active self-seeking; inner righteousness vs. inner unrighteousness; emptiness (rest) + desire (work) → righteousness (mutuality, union)
- *Practice*: rest

11

THE TREASURE OF BEING GOD WITH GOD

Alice laughed. "There's no use trying," she said. "One can't believe
impossible things."
"I daresay you haven't had much practice," said the Queen. "When I
was your age, I always did it for half an hour a day. Why, sometimes I've
believed as many as six impossible things before breakfast."

—Lewis Carroll, *Through the Looking-Glass*

A ND NOW FOR SOMETHING completely different. Or, considering our
journey so far, perhaps it's not so different after all. It might actually
seem like the next logical step. But it's a step into a realm—into a life—unlike anything we could ever dream up. And yet it is real . . . very real . . . the
most real. It is the ground of reality itself. But like so many things that are
more real than what we're used to, it might require some imagination in
order for us to begin to wrap our minds around it.

In *Through the Looking-Glass*, young Alice looks into a large mirror
and finds that she is able to step into the different world revealed on the
other side. There she finds a place where things are backward and all very
strange and very alive with fantastical characters. At one point, two such
characters, Tweedledum and Tweedledee, direct Alice's attention to the Red
King, who is snoring in deep sleep. The twins wonder aloud to Alice if
she might actually exist only as an imaginary figure in the king's dreams.
It's a thought that still haunts Alice when she finally returns to her world.
Which one is real, Alice wonders, her world or the world through the looking glass?

We have come to a place on our journey in which Alice's adventure might prove informative, though we must adapt it to our own situation. Imagine Alice looking into the mirror. She sees her own image reflected back. There now appears to be two Alices: the original Alice and the imaged Alice. Now imagine that Imaged Alice actually has consciousness and a life in the world on the other side of the mirror. She sees the other Alice looking at her, and sometimes Imaged Alice even wonders if *she* might be the Original Alice and the other one is only *her* reflection.

But then something happens that answers that potential misperception. One day, Original Alice reaches out and begins removing the mirror from the wall. Imaged Alice grasps for her bearings, desperately afraid that her world is about to disappear, and she right along with it. But, to her awestruck surprise, with the mirror removed she now finds herself looking out through the eyes of Original Alice. Imaged Alice still has her own consciousness, and she is aware that she and Original Alice are still two different beings. Only now, there is no mirror between them.

Imaged Alice can now see her old reality and her strange new reality, which is actually the *real* reality, as Original Alice sees it. What's more, now that they are fully one, Imaged Alice can see and know Original Alice as Original Alice sees and knows herself . . . at least much more than before. And because of all this, Imaged Alice is able to become so much more like Original Alice that there is almost no distinction between them. Oh, she never actually *becomes* Original Alice. She retains her own consciousness; but because of her new and vaster perspective, what it means to be Imaged Alice takes on profound new dimensions. And through it all, she is content and even amazed to simply be Alice with Alice.

This might all seem very strange and fantastical. And indeed it is! But this, dear friend and fellow Imaged Alice, is the Contemplative Life.

Raiders of the Lost Teaching

The reason such a consideration—that the imaged might become so united with its original that the two become practically indistinct—is strange to many of us is because we are largely unfamiliar with the doctrine of *deification* (also known as *theosis* and *divinization*). It is a fundamental doctrine in Orthodoxy and the Christian East, as seen, for example, in the teaching of pioneering theologian Athanasius of Alexandria (ca. 296–373): God became human so that we humans might become God.[1]

It seems shocking, especially for those who think of the gospel only in terms of being saved *from* sin and hell, without much thought of being saved *for* Christlikeness and all the ramifications of that term. But what is it to be Christlike if not to be Godlike? Indeed, the doctrine of deification has its roots in Jesus's own teaching. For example, when Jewish leaders are taking up stones to kill Jesus for claiming to be one with God, whom he calls Father, he defends himself with Scripture: "Is it not written in your Law, 'I have said you are gods'?" (John 10:34).[2]

Not only does Jesus not go on to explain away this verse, he doubles down on it, claiming that if God calls his people "gods," how much more appropriate is it that his only begotten Son should have that designation. Another beautiful example is found in Jesus's high priestly prayer: "I pray that all of them may be one, Father, just as you are in me and I am in you. May they also be in us" (John 17:21). How could someone be "in" the divine Father and Son—and "just as" they are "in" each other—without being touched with some amount of divinity?

Christ's first followers embraced this idea of transformative, deifying union as well, for example in 2 Peter:

> His divine power has given us everything we need *for a godly life* through our knowledge of him who called us by his own glory and goodness. Through these he has given us his very great and precious promises, so that through them *you may participate in the divine nature*, having escaped the corruption in the world caused by evil desires. (2 Pet 1:3–4; emphases added)

Though we have tamed the word "godly" to mean something like "respectable," its juxtaposition here with the claim that "you may participate in the divine nature" indicates that "godly" can mean nothing less than "Godlike." It is to partake of the very *nature* of God, which is to say, to share in God's God-ness.

This teaching was largely embraced and developed in the Christian East, as articulated in the above quote from Athanasius. His predecessor, Origen of Alexandria (ca. 185–254), likewise explained,

---

1. Alternatively translated with a lower case, "humans might be made god" (Greek *theopoiēthōmen*). Athanasius of Alexandria, *Inc.* 54.3.

2. See Ps 82:6: "I say, 'You are gods, children of the Most High, all of you.'"

Christians see that with Jesus human and divine nature began to be woven together, so that by fellowship with divinity human nature might become divine, not only in Jesus, but also in all those who believe and go on to undertake the life which Jesus taught, the life which leads everyone who lives according to Jesus' commandments to friendship with God and fellowship with Jesus.[3]

Later, Maximus the Confessor (ca. 580–662), "the last common Father of both East and West," presented his understanding of "salvation through Christ primarily as deification."[4] He presented a path of spiritual growth as participation in the simultaneously transcendent and immanent life of God so complete and transformational that one eventually "becomes God by deification."[5] Maximus is clear, however, that "never can a soul reach out toward the knowledge of God if God himself does not, having condescended, lay hold of it and lead it up to himself," and that "God is the fashioner of all life, immortality, holiness, and virtue."[6]

As with other aspects of Eastern Christianity, deification has often been considered questionable and even suspicious in the Christian West, with its roots in the Roman legal tradition and emphases on things like justification, often thought of in penal terms of guilt or innocence and right standing before God as Judge. However, even Augustine taught that

> God, you see, wants to make you a god; not by nature, of course, like the one whom he begot; but by his gift and by adoption. For just as he who through being humbled came to share your mortality; so through lifting you up he brings you to share his immortality . . . and thus the whole man being deified [Latin *homo deificatus*] and made divine may cleave forever to the everlasting and unchangeable truth.[7]

Despite such insights, however, this vital doctrine never really gained a significant place in Western theology.

The Wesleyan-Methodist tradition eventually got close to deification with its teaching on "Christian perfection" and "entire sanctification." This is essentially the belief that full cooperation with God's grace can actually lead in this life to perfect (i.e., total, not lacking) love for God with one's

3. Origen, *Cels.* 3.29.

4. McGinn, *Essential Writings*, 408.

5. Maximus the Confessor, *Two Hundred Chapters*, 1.54.

6. Maximus the Confessor, *Two Hundred Chapters*, 1.31, 1.50.

7. Augustine, *Serm.* 166.4.

entire being—all the heart, mind, soul, and strength (Mark 12:30). This would also include love for all that God loves. The teaching takes seriously the witness, promises, and expectations of Christ and the early church: to "be perfect, therefore, as your heavenly Father is perfect" (Matt 5:48); that God will "sanctify you entirely . . . your spirit and soul and body kept sound and blameless" (1 Thess 5:23 NRSV); that we should "go on toward perfection" (Heb 6:1); that "love is perfected in us" so that "In this world we are like Jesus" (1 John 4:17); and so on.[8]

Others have emphasized holiness and even Christlikeness, but it has often (though not always) been a rather superficial and toothless teaching of a "What would Jesus do?" variety, rather than living the actual life of Christ from the inside out. Instead, deification has largely been relegated to the oft-misunderstood and neglected realm of mystical theology (which for Eastern Christianity is simply theology, with no real distinction between mystical and otherwise). A more expansive exploration of the doctrine and its history can be left for another time and place.[9] We'll assume that if we've come this far on our journey, we're prepared to continue on to Ruusbroec's treatment of deification in what he calls the Contemplative Life.

Like many other mystical theologians, Reverend John ran afoul of some religious authorities in late-medieval Western Christendom because of his teaching on the subject, damaging his reputation for generations after his death. And, honestly, it is an easily misunderstood doctrine. Reverend John's *Little Book of Enlightenment* (also called *Little Book of Clarification*) was actually written for some monks who were struggling with his teaching on deification, what he called Union without Difference (or Distinction). This was the community he visited and discovered that they had a bootlegged copy of his first, unpublished book. He made no apologies for his teaching, but he did write the short book to help clarify things.

As we'll see, the Contemplative Life does need clarification, though it can only really be grasped by living it. As Thomas Merton noted, "Contemplation cannot be taught. It cannot even be clearly explained. It can only

8. See Wesley, *Plain Account of Christian Perfection*. The doctrine includes love for neighbor, of course, articulated as "social holiness," which connotes relationships for accountability and growth, as well as sociocultural change. Sins of ignorance, the ramifications of sin, and backsliding remain realities and possibilities. Still, the doctrine is thoroughly grounded in Christ's teaching, but it is (unfortunately) largely unique in Protestantism. For a good and readable survey, see Watson, *Perfect Love*. I also explore this in Pelfrey, *Still Moving*.

9. See, for example, Payton, *Light from Christian East*; and Lossky, *Mystical Theology*.

be hinted at, suggested, pointed to, symbolized."[10] This is why the section on the Contemplative Life is the shortest section in Ruusbroec's *Spiritual Espousals*, and only one chapter in this book. We are now well into the area of "speculative theology," which is grounded in Scripture and theological tradition, of course, but is attempting to examine and describe the largely indescribable. We can be sure that the reality is far more awesome and mystifying than anything we are presently attempting to understand. However, considering the ground we've covered on our journey, it should be no surprise that to go even higher and deeper into our union with God will require continued letting go of the need to understand everything. And so, on we go . . . through the looking glass.

Through the Looking Glass: The Contemplative Life

It is probably clear from our little story that Original Alice is God, and we are Imaged Alice. As we explored earlier, we are like a magic mirror in which God is imaged and reflected—to ourselves, to our neighbors and the natural world, and back to God in worship. In Reverend John's theology, God the Son is the actual Image of God, and humans are made *to* that Image. We are images of the Image. So, as our journey has led us to become more and more like Christ our Helper and Mentor, it has resulted in our becoming a clearer and more faithful image of God.

We have become so completely united with Christ our Bridegroom and so fully held in the embrace of the divine Trinity and Unity that we no longer require a go-between. God has reached out and removed the mirror, so that now, as Reverend John says, we can see and contemplate "God with God, without intermediary or any otherness which can create a hindrance or a mediation."[11] What we struggled for unsuccessfully way back in our Quest for the Essence with its storm of love—to remove even a paper-thin distance in order to experience God *with God*—is finally ready to be realized here in the Contemplative Life.

We should first be clear that "contemplative" does not indicate something like being in a trance or the previously discussed "false emptiness" or other misconceptions we might have picked up. As we'll see, to contemplate is to participate in, and to be an expression of, the life of the Trinity. As Merton explains, "Contemplation is also the response to a call: a call from

10. Merton, *New Seeds of Contemplation*, 6.
11. John of Ruusbroec, *Spiritual Espousals*, c29–31.

Him Who has no voice, and yet Who speaks in everything that is, and Who, most of all, speaks in the depths of our own being: for we ourselves are words of His . . . He answers Himself in us and this answer is divine life, divine creativity, making all things new."[12]

Merton here is referring to another classic way of speaking of Christ, as Word of God (John 1:1). For example, when we read or hear the word "tree" or "bicycle," we immediately think of the thing the word indicates, rather than thinking of the shape or sound of the letters (though there can be beauty and importance there too). So, Christ as Word of God is another way of describing Christ as Image of God, as the creative and creating— though not created—expression of the thing indicated. Similarly, we are words of God, created and creative expressions of the divine.[13] We are (in the Greek) *logoi* of the *Logos*. God "answers Himself in us and this answer is divine life."

The settings and landscapes of the journey so far have included sunny mountaintops, cool valleys, a kingdom and its citizens, oppressively arid plains, refreshing streams, a flooding fountain and its deep origins, and more. But the landscape of the Contemplative Life is stark simplicity: darkness and light. All is stripped away and the focus is solely on the divine Trinity in its divine Unity. And we are there, within their union, living the Contemplative Life.

We have descended to the deepest recesses of the kingdom of the soul, of our overall journey, and even of eternity. The experience of being united with such pure, true light requires a type of annihilation, which can initially feel hellish as it requires a letting go even of our image-bound conception of God. Most heroic journeys necessarily lead through some expression of an underworld, some point of ultimate letting go, not only of ourselves (which began way back at the First Threshold) but even of what we thought we knew of God.

We are at a state of union that cannot be attained by acts of will, but is really only the result of having journeyed this far. Even Reverend John is less a guide here and more the narrator of a story that must be experienced to be understood, if understanding is ever even possible, as he explains of his own teaching here, "No one will really thoroughly understand these remarks by means of any study or subtle consideration on one's own. For all the words and everything that one can learn and understand in a creaturely

12. Merton, *New Seeds of Contemplation*, 3.
13. For more on this, see Mulholland, *Shaped by the Word*.

fashion is alien to, and far beneath, the truth that I have in mind."[14] Our best bet, then, is to stick with our familiar image and mystical earworm—"See, the bridegroom comes! Go out to meet him!"—and to make the road by walking it.

See: Darkness in Light

As we travel through the Contemplative Life, we again walk the roads of purgation and illumination, leading to the ultimate *via unitiva* (way of union). Here we must be purged of worldly and creaturely works, attachments, and even our notions of self. This purgation is necessary to hear the Father speaking a deep and mysterious word in the hidden parts of our soul, a word in which the Father speaks himself and all things. This word is "See," and our heavenly Father speaks it because he wishes us to be seeing, because God is the Father of light. But we are not yet able to see here. The light is too dazzling, and what it reveals is too awesome for us to comprehend. Still, the word is being spoken.

In order to see in that light, we must first lose ourselves in this state of living in a deep darkness without an intermediary between us and God. It is a state in which all contemplatives wander around in enjoyment and can no longer find themselves in a creaturely (i.e., fleshly, worldly) way. It is an abyss of darkness in which we as loving spirits have died to ourselves— particularly our false selves—that we might find our true selves fully alive in God. This is the final mysterious letting go in which we are purged of creaturely dependencies and are abandoned to God. We must simply *be*. And we must rest in the faith of our simple being within God's simple being, and God's being within ours.

The darkness of this death is like an embryonic darkness, "for in this darkness there shines and is born an incomprehensible light which is the Son of God, in whom one contemplates eternal life. And in this light one becomes seeing."[15] Here Reverend John juxtaposes apparent opposites, drawing on non-dual thinking, in an attempt to communicate the incomprehensible: light from darkness, birth from death, sight in hiddenness, and the contemplation of emptiness. Perhaps the most profound juxtaposition is the recognition of the divine within the creature, as this light that we receive in the midst of our simple being is actually God. Yet we do not stop

14. John of Ruusbroec, *Spiritual Espousals*, c23–27.
15. John of Ruusbroec, *Spiritual Espousals*, c56–59.

with our being merely receiving God. The process is constant and transformative. Without intermediary and without cease our being becomes the very brightness it receives. So it is that we "who with unveiled faces contemplate the Lord's glory, are being transformed into his image with ever-increasing glory" (2 Cor 3:18). To see in this way is to possess eternal life.

The Bridegroom Comes: A Hidden Revelation in the Eternal Now

In the exact moment of our seeing, we behold the coming of Christ our Bridegroom. That is the *what* of our seeing. Reverend John uses a pair of apparent contradictions, again requiring non-dual thinking, in an attempt to explain this coming. First, the coming of the Bridegroom in the Contemplative Life occurs in *the eternal now.*[16] We might think of "eternity" as meaning time extending forever into the future and the past. But eternity is actually a wholly different state of existence from our space-time way of thinking. Yes, it extends forever into the past and forever into the future, although "past" and "future" are relative concepts that have little relevance for understanding eternity.

Eternal life is far more a *quality* of life than a *quantity.* The Greek—*aiōnios zoē* (e.g., John 17:3)—literally means "age-quality life" or "life of the age," which in the New Testament context indicated life in God's kingdom that was ushered in with and characterized Jesus's ministry. This is what is meant by "eternal life" in passages like John 3:16. God's love for the world results in God the Son coming to welcome us into eternal life—not just unending life in the hereafter, but the everlasting life of God in the here and now. God comes to gather everyone and everything into divine unity (see Eph 1:10). Jesus defines eternal life as knowing the only true God and knowing Jesus Christ, whom God sent (John 17:3). Note the emphasis on "knowing," with the picture of eternal life as sharing in fellowship (*koinōnia*) with God. So, "the eternal now" is the unfathomable being and holy company of God moving into our humble lives right here where we are and as we are . . . again and again.

In a series of verbal gymnastics, Reverend John strains to describe how "the coming of the Bridegroom is so rapid that He is always having come and is indwelling with fathomless richness, and that He is coming anew personally, without cease, with such new brightness just as though He

---

16. John of Ruusbroec, *Spiritual Espousals*, c85.

had never come before."[17] We need to break that down. The eternal now is something like Christ's coming in the past and in the future rushing together into the present, fresh and bright within us in every new, life-giving moment, full to overflowing with the richness of heaven and of God's own being.[18] To see the coming of the Bridegroom in the eternal now is to gaze *at* the light, *with* the light, *in* the light.

The second seemingly contradictory (non-dual) description of contemplating the coming of the Bridegroom is that it is the *hidden revelation* of God.[19] An oxymoron like "hidden revelation" only begins to make sense at this point in our journey. We have reached this state of deep light, of hidden brightness, in which everything is stripped away and we contemplate God as all we could ever want. And the ground from which this brightness shines, which is actually God as the Ground of all being, is alive and fruitful like fertile farmland. So, like cultivated soil turned over and nourished, this land of eternal light is constantly renewed and ready in the hidden depths of our being, ready to bear fruit that brings the life of heaven into the world around us. It is both hidden and revealed. The life contemplating the coming Bridegroom is like a door that opens into the eternally vast expanse of the heavenly country that is God.

This is the experience of illumination that follows the purgation of being lost in the dark in the "seeing" stage. Having first learned to un-see, now we are able to see. In fact, this illumination is the opposite of that blinding purgation, for the eyes of our being that contemplate and gaze upon our Bridegroom are so wide open now that they will never again be closed. Even more, the arms of our being are so wide open to embrace the coming of our Bridegroom that our being itself has become the wideness of the embrace. Like a bride and groom standing together at the altar, the two embarking on a new life as one (yet still distinct), we have entered a deeply profound experience of becoming, seen in these ideas of our *becoming* the brightness we receive and *becoming* the wideness we embrace. The only thing left for us to become is exactly where we go next: *becoming* God with God.

17. John of Ruusbroec, *Spiritual Espousals*, c81–84.

18. This reach into the past and the future in the midst of the present is akin to what Kurt Vonnegut, in *Slaughterhouse-Five*, calls "coming unstuck in time." Of course, Vonnegut and Ruusbroec are approaching it from very different perspectives! Still, it's fun (for me anyway) to think of "the eternal now" as "coming unstuck in time," but with God.

19. John of Ruusbroec, *Spiritual Espousals*, c91.

META UNION: God with God

The likely reason this leg of our journey is so strange and confusing is that it takes place within the embrace of the Holy Trinity. And now, the looking glass having been removed, we are exploring the state of "superessential union," which is to say, union *above* the essence of our being that we've come to know as "soul" and its rootedness in God. We'll recall that our first experience of union with God is Natural Union. And our second and third experiences of union are Supernatural Union *with* Intermediary and Supernatural Union *without* Intermediary. Each of these experiences of divine union does not go away but is swallowed in the next.

This fourth and ultimate experience of union is what Reverend John calls Union without Difference, alternatively translated as Union without Distinction. It should be understood as superessential union, that is, union above ("super") the essence ("essential") of our being. If we cheekily designated supernatural union as Super Union!, this superessential union might be considered META UNION, since it transcends and informs being itself. So, META UNION is union as God with God . . . without difference or distinction . . . and beyond being . . . whew!

Now we are wandering in the indescribable country of the intra-Trinitarian dynamics, which is to say, the life of the Persons of the Trinity among themselves. This is the Reality of realities and the Life of lives. We must steel ourselves and tread very carefully, spiritual eyes and spiritual arms and spiritual mind wide open. And we should remember that this is not something we are trying to attain. This is something that simply is, and we are learning to be with it.

Reverend John's explanation of this territory is based on the respective role of each divine Person, which in turn gives rise to our anthropology and our basis for participating in the divine nature. Here, our narrator pulls back the curtain, revealing the driving force behind our entire journey. As the goal of our search, this superessential META UNION and the Trinitarian workings behind it are the "place" at which we have presently arrived. It is best to let our guide offer the details in his own words:

> Here there spring forth and begin an eternal going-out and an eternal activity without beginning. For here there is a beginning without beginning. For as the almighty Father has perfectly comprehended Himself in the ground of His fruitfulness, [so] the Son, the eternal Word of the Father, has gone out, as another person in the Godhead. And through the eternal birth all creatures have

gone out eternally, before they were created in time. Thus God has beheld them and known them in Himself, with distinction, in life-giving ideas, and in otherness from Himself; but they are not other in every respect: for all that is in God is God. This eternal going-out, this eternal life which we have and are within God, eternally, outside ourselves, is the cause of our created being in time.[20]

This is shocking and baffling stuff! But how could the life of the divine Trinity be otherwise? Now, lest we get overwhelmed by the barrage of mystical concepts, let's take this apart a bit. These are some of the key theological underpinnings of the formational journey we're on (and of all of Christian theology). We see here that the Father is the fruitful Ground from which the Son, the Word, eternally goes forth. Yet we also revisit our anthropology and ontology that we explored at the beginning of the long journey through the Inner Life, how the nature of humanity is essentially united with God, even prior to our created being in time. Now we look at that again, seeing the true nature of our being as the basis for our deification (Godlikeness) and our META UNION (union above our essence in God). It is the basis for living as God with God. Reverend John is careful to note that creatures are distinct and "other" from God, though not in every respect, "for all that is in God is God."

This is a confusing and potentially dangerous teaching, and Ruusbroec takes care to avoid going as far down this road as some other mystics do. Some, like Meister Eckhart (ca. 1260–1328), paid for it with their reputations, while others, like Marguerite Porete (d. 1310), paid for it with their lives. Our participation in the divine nature and experience of "eternal life" are not the result of some mystical achievement on our part, by which we literally become Christ or God. Instead, our life—and life itself—is an idea God had and keeps having, which God willed to bring into being, and which God sustains through and calls to union with himself, though we remain distinct beings. And this whole life and movement finds its origins in the eternal birth, or "going out," of God the Son.

Go Out: Transformed in the Trinitarian Embrace

This is where we now find ourselves, "going out" to behold God with God, to move with the Son, who is the Image of the Holy Trinity, back into the fruitful Ground of eternal being in the Godhead, which we might understand as

20. John of Ruusbroec, *Spiritual Espousals*, c108–17.

the divine Unity and the essence of God's God-ness. This, says Ruusbroec, is "the bosom of the Father," which is "our own ground and our origin, in which we begin our life and our being."[21] So, the Son is united with the Father in the dark Ground of the Godhead, while simultaneously he is born in an eternal brightness. And because this is the state of the Son, the divine Image, it is also the state of those who are made to that Image, us. For everything that the Father is and has, he gives to the Son (except Fatherhood, which by definition is the Father's alone). And therefore, everything that lives united and unseen in the Father, lives united and revealed in the Son. And somewhere in that beautiful, mysterious, loving mix, we find ourselves . . . even as we lose ourselves.

It seems that this is our nature, which is to say the nature of all humans clothed with (participating in) God's transforming grace. Yet it is only through the formational journey that we discover this reality and are able to comprehend our own identity made to the divine Image. However, as we journey (and are carried) to this point above ourselves in the brightness of the Trinitarian embrace, we see ourselves as one with that brightness. It is by the illumination of this brightness that we are able to see that we are part of that same Ground out of which the brightness shines. In the way that God looks at us and somehow sees himself looking back, so now we look at God and somehow see our true selves looking back.

So, our calling at this stage is to go out in contemplation—above reason, above any distinction between us and God, and above our created being—with eternal inward focus through the inborn light. Thus we are transformed and are at one with that same light by which we see, and which we see. This is Reverend John's extraordinary description of illumination, that we now *see* the divine light, see *by* the divine light, and see *as* the divine light. Here we move past the misguided quest for physical immortality, exchanging a narrow focus on our body and personality for a much larger, unobstructed vision of immortality as a present fact. The vision is of the mutual movement and superessential (i.e., in the realm of God's God-ness) uniting of us as bride with the Son-of-God Bridegroom. We are married to the unending Life of life.

This is what it is to live as God with God. It is as if we are walking around the vast landscape of darkness and light and piecing together a description of this highest experience of unity. We have considered how we *are* the wideness of the landscape, we *are* the brightness, and we *are*

---

21. John of Ruusbroec, *Spiritual Espousals*, c136–37.

the ground from which the light comes. So, what we in the Contemplative Life are now beginning to realize is that this landscape *is* God. And what is happening is that we are moving into the eternal Image to which we were made, and we are contemplating God and all things without distinction in a united seeing by way of this divine brightness.

Perhaps we have used expressions like "life with God" without really considering the implications of such a state. But this really is life *with God*, seeing God and all things from within God. (Remember Imaged Alice seeing everything as Original Alice?) It is likely that we underestimated what Jesus meant by saying his disciples should be baptized "in the name of the Father and of the Son and of the Holy Spirit" (Matt 28:19). Far more than a simple ritual and liturgy, this is full immersion into a wholly different reality defined and characterized by the life of the Trinity.

This is the highest and most fruitful experience of contemplation we can have in this life, for the Contemplative Life is a heavenly life. In this divine landscape—this stage of being elevated above our creaturely state—we experience true freedom, self-mastery, and potential for growth in a sublime life beyond all that we can understand. Amazingly, though understandably, there is still more growth and brightness and nobility to be had in life beyond our present bodily existence. Nevertheless, we have now obtained and are living into the glory of our journey's greatest treasure: Union without Difference, META UNION, the highest state of union with God. Where we previously obtained the treasure of unmediated union with God, we are now experiencing its transformational powers in all aspects of our life . . . aspects that we probably didn't even realize were part of our life. We are transformed in the Trinitarian embrace as if cloaked in a royal robe and beginning to comprehend and live out its royal implications.

To Meet Him: Finding Ourselves in Love

Here is where the inner workings of the Trinity are most explicitly revealed. We have discovered unity in the bosom of the Father as the dark, fruitful Ground, and with the ceaseless birth of the Son in the bright revelation of the eternal now. But what of the third divine Person? The Holy Spirit has made occasional appearances in our narrative, but is seemingly elusive and distant, passing through but mostly calling from the wings. Now, however, emerging from the divine dark resplendence, the Spirit takes center stage.

Reverend John tells of a "loving meeting in which, above all, our supreme blessedness consists."[22] Surely, we think, our guide must be speaking of the meeting between us and our long-sought-after Bridegroom. Yet
there is something more—something so much more that the entire journey
seems to shift significantly. Suddenly, *we* slide into the shadows of what was
thought to be our own story, and the true drama unfolds. Reverend John
looks over his shoulder at us and whispers to us as both his bewildered
students and awestruck fellow travelers:

> You should know that the heavenly Father, as a living ground,
> with all that is living in Him, is actively turned towards His Son as
> towards His own eternal Wisdom; and the same Wisdom and all
> that is living within it is actively turned back towards the Father,
> that is, towards the same ground whence it comes. And in this
> meeting there springs forth the third Person, between the Father
> and the Son, that is, the Holy Spirit, their mutual love, who is one
> with them both in the same nature.[23]

Far from a bit player or distant participant, the Holy Spirit is the divine
Person manifesting the love of Father and Son and all that is living in them.
We do well to notice that repeated phrase "and all that is living within"
the Trinity, for that includes us (and likely much more). Early on we were
taught that humility is the foundational virtue, and perhaps now we understand why: we cannot help but be profoundly humbled at this revelation.
For the Love who is the Holy Spirit "actively and enjoyably encompasses
and pervades the Father, the Son, and everything that is living in both of
them with such great richness and joy that all creatures must eternally keep
silent about it. For the incomprehensible marvel which resides in this love
eternally transcends all creatures' understanding."[24]

Our silence here is the result of our exalted state of contemplating the
union of Father and Son in the Love who is the Holy Spirit. And we are
also dumbstruck by finding our own being above ourselves and one with
the Spirit of God, where we taste and see without measure—even as God
with God—the richness of our unity in the living Ground where we live
life above the creaturely way we've always experienced it. We have passed
beyond the images and symbols of our mythology, the stories that have
tried to communicate truths beyond words. Even a concept like "Father,

22. John of Ruusbroec, *Spiritual Espousals*, c182–83.

23. John of Ruusbroec, *Spiritual Espousals*, c183–89.

24. John of Ruusbroec, *Spiritual Espousals*, c190–93.

Son, and Holy Spirit" is surely insufficient in capturing the reality.[25] We have come to the hidden place where only awestruck silence remains.

This is the blissful meeting, the state in which God's way of being becomes our way of being. Despite the insufficiency of the language, this is what we have to work with, and it is quite revealing and even moving:

> For just as the Father beholds all things anew, without cease, in the birth of His Son, thus all things are loved anew by the Father and by the Son in the outflowing of the Holy Spirit. And this is the active meeting of the Father and of the Son, in which we are lovingly embraced, through the Holy Spirit, in eternal love.[26]

So we have not only been united with our beloved and sought-after Bridegroom (the Son), but also with the Bridegroom's Father and the Holy Spirit, who is the active power and divine Person of Love itself. The Holy Spirit is, in fact, the divine Agent who brings us into this Trinitarian embrace.

Though we are still creatures, we are now united with God without apparent difference or distinction between us, as our creatureliness is caught up and transformed in the eternal embrace of the divine Unity with the Persons of the divine Trinity. We are shocked to get even a hint of a fuller glimpse of who God really is. Far from some cartoonish "old man in the sky," God is understood here as dynamic interrelatedness and vibrant love, eternally wise yet endlessly fruitful and new. Within all this, we are almost equally shocked to get a glimpse of who we really are. And who knew that by finding the one (God as Unity and Trinity), we would find the other (our true selves)?

Way-Stop #11: Reflection

Our minds are probably reeling at this point. This section might have contained too much mysticism even for eager mystics. It might be helpful

---

25. Scripture itself tells us that the image of God is both male and female (Gen 1:27), and the picture of God giving birth certainly must include God as Mother (e.g., Deut 32:18; Isa 42:14; 66:13). There are surely reasons far beyond the scope of this footnote that God is understood to have revealed himself as Father, Son, and Holy Spirit—or more broadly as Parent, Begotten Offspring, and Spirit—but even the biblical record indicates that there is much more to the picture. For an insightful and fresh perspective, see Coakley, *God, Sexuality and Self*.

26. John of Ruusbroec, *Spiritual Espousals*, c202–6.

to get primitive for a moment, to go back to the beginning . . . the very beginning. We mentioned back in the first chapter that part of the initial situation of our journey is the ongoing ramifications of so-called original sin, the mess between our first human parents and the serpent and the lie that we can become like God *without* God (Gen 3:5). In addition to believing the same lie, we also tend to share their response of shame, finding various ways to hide from God and from our true selves (3:7–10). So, this Contemplative Life and META UNION are basically about rediscovering our original blessedness, getting back in step with God and God's plan that we are indeed made to be like God (1:27–28), but we can only truly do so *with God*: what Reverend John calls "contemplating God with God."

The best practice we can take up in this stage is likely the classic Benedictine discipline of manual labor. While contemplative, meditative prayer is certainly appropriate and vital here (including *lectio divina*, breath prayers, etc.), it is also important to remember that the Contemplative Life is still an embodied life. Therefore, things like working in the garden, washing dishes, taking walks and exercising, knitting, playing a musical instrument, and the like can be helpful in what Brother Lawrence (ca. 1614–91)—whose primary monastic duties included working in the kitchen and repairing sandals—called "practicing the presence of God." The body and mind can be distractedly engaged while the soul rests in the divine embrace.

And thus, with the Contemplative Life, our search is over. We have found and examined and are coming to fully live out the four ways of experiencing our great treasure of union with God. We might think of this section as a four-episode television show called *The Treasure*, since what we've been looking at are four parts of one whole: Part 1, Natural Union; Part 2, Supernatural Union with Intermediary; Part 3, Supernatural Union without Intermediary; Part 4, Union without Difference. Our series finale was certainly a must-see event! We finally and fully found our Bridegroom. We have been joined in spiritual marriage. The veil has been lifted and we are, to quote Reverend John, "lovingly embraced in eternal love." Who knew mysticism was so romantic!

Whatever separated us from God—the bad and even the good—has been removed, so that now we can live as participants in the life of God and even share in the divine nature, in God's God-ness. After all our searching and longing and struggling to let go, we are finally at rest in the secure and loving and joyful embrace of God, a union that has no beginning and no end and, to be honest, no need of us . . . yet here we are. What does this mean, really? Can we handle it? It's all just so much! Is this the end? Have we arrived? Surely there can't be more.

The truth is, we have indeed come to the end of the long Road of our inner journey, which turned out to stretch from the Inner Life on through the Contemplative Life. Huzzah! But have we arrived? Far from it. We've gone the right way through the looking glass, now experiencing life and God and reality *with God*. However, the bizarro world that we originally inhabited is still strange and backward and utterly convinced that its way is what's real, and that the life we have now entered into is so much fantasy and myth and wishful thinking.

Will we turn our backs on that world, letting it fend for itself while we lose ourselves in the newlywed life of divine union? If we have truly been crowned with deification—which is to say, if we are participating in the nature and life of the God incarnated and revealed in Jesus Christ—then the answer should be clear.

Bearings

◆ *Location*: the Road (the Treasure) > the Contemplative Life > "See, the bridegroom comes; go out to meet him."

◆ *Key Concepts*: deification; *via unitiva*; the eternal now; Superessential Union—Union without Difference/Distinction, contemplating God with God; the Father as Ground of being, the Son as divine Exemplar (Image, Word, Wisdom), and the Holy Spirit as divine Love and Agent of union

◆ *Practice*: manual labor (plus contemplative practices)

Part IV

THE RETURN

12

THE CALL TO RETURN

Robert Kennedy, whose summer house is eight miles from the home
I live in all year round, was shot two nights ago. He died last night. So
it goes. Martin Luther King was shot a month ago. He died, too. So it
goes. . . . My father died many years ago now—of natural causes. So it
goes. He was a sweet man. He was a gun nut, too. He left me his guns.
They rust.

—Kurt Vonnegut Jr., *Slaughterhouse-Five*

N OW WHAT? OUR QUESTIONS have been answered. There is more to
life—far more to life than what we find in the world's hollow promises and our own humdrum goings on. There is more to us—far more to
us than the fleshy figure we see in the mirror and the roles we play as we
strut and fret upon life's stage. There is worth—treasure far greater than the
mirage of material wealth and delusions of grandeur that we sacrifice our
souls to gain, only to find slipping like sand through our fingers. Perhaps
without our realizing it we have grappled with some of the profoundest
issues of philosophy, psychology, theology, and more; and we have found
those issues answered in an embrace. Our existential angst and yearning
have found their satisfaction in essential Love, our longings for meaning
now rooted and fruitful in the eternal Ground of being.

And still . . . so it goes.

Now what? It might seem like an indulgent new question to ask, especially in light of all we've been through. We have come to the end of
the Road, gained a treasure beyond imagining, and been enrobed with the

glory and honor of deified royalty. We have set foot in Aslan's Country and knelt before the transforming presence of the Emperor-beyond-the-Sea. We have been given a glimpse behind Oz's curtain and, instead of the reality being less than the myths, it is so infinitely more that it leaves us forever changed and grasping wildly for the right metaphor to convey even a fraction of what we've encountered. We have become one with the Force that creates and permeates and gives life to every colossal and miniscule thing in the universe, in all the universes, and yet is personal and joyous and loving and transcends it all.

So now what? More than indulgent, the question might seem absurd in light of the context of our journey. Do we really expect there to be more? If this is all true—that we are called to a reality-altering adventure and we can have Christ for a Helper and Teacher, that our very being is united with God and all aspects of our life can be supernaturally transformed, that every moment is shot through with the eternal presence of the Triune God and that we are held and loved and empowered and even deified in that presence—then what else could we hope for?

The reason "Now what?" is not an absurd question is that there is indeed more. We should probably be careful what we wish for, because the journey does continue. Do we really want it to? It's quite possible that we are overwhelmed by the journey so far. We might wonder what all of this mystical-heroic stuff has to do with our everyday lives. Such high-minded ideas have no place in the grit and mud and confusing compromises and contradictions of this world. The mysteries of the divine Unity and Trinity are better left to a few scattered mountaintops and monasteries and seminary classrooms and the afterlife. Even now, we might be arguing with ourselves that this is all too good and mysterious and complicated to be real. We should just slip back into our identity as sinners waiting for heaven, fallen but "saved" just enough to get past the velvet rope when we die. Or atheism, hedonism, apathy, and despair are always options as well.

If I may take a moment of authorial privilege, I must say that I get it. I understand that this journey isn't easy. I spent years researching this material and wrote dozens of drafts on it for my doctoral thesis. Then I wrote more drafts as I prepared that work for publication as a scholarly monograph. Now I've written and rewritten draft after draft of this book so I can share this teaching with you. And with every jot and tittle, every day spent grappling with this mystical-heroic theology of spiritual formation, I continue to learn. This stuff is dense and complex, and it takes time and effort to understand. I might suggest, in all humility, that this book will likely need to be reread once you've gotten through this final section. I hope revisiting the journey will help you as it continues to help me. At some point you might want to dive in to the primary sources and take on John of Ruusbroec *mano a mano*.[1] Whatever it takes, I can attest that it's worth it. It is *so* worth it. But it isn't easy . . . heroism never is.

On the other hand, and perhaps worse than telling ourselves that this is all too much to get, we might be telling ourselves we've arrived. We have gained some secret knowledge that entitles us to our own private experience of God—no more need for those earlier things like disciplines and virtues and community. And certainly no need to go back to the world we left behind when we answered the Call to this adventure.

The problem with all of this muddled thinking is Jesus. Regarding this notion of leaving the world and others behind, we don't get to relish the idea of deification while despising Christ's muddy, bloody incarnation. If God looks like Jesus, and Godlikeness looks like Christlikeness, then that's going to mean sacrificing ourselves in love, which is messy business.

Alternatively, regarding the temptation to chuck all this lofty teaching in exchange for something a bit less challenging, we shouldn't make the foolish error of mistaking Jesus for just another guru spouting bumper-sticker maxims—some wise stuff about loving neighbors and doing unto others, mixed with some crazy stuff about God being his Father and the Spirit of truth coming to teach people about him and being born again from above. No, if we are following him on this sprawling adventure, then Christ must be *both* our Son-of-God exemplar of divinity *and* our incarnated Master in the school of the kingdom of the soul. We can't have one without the other, nor can we pick and choose which teachings and characteristics of godliness suit us and which we'll disregard.

Instead, "let the same mind be in you that was in Christ Jesus, who, though he was in the form of God, did not regard equality with God as something to be exploited, but emptied himself, taking the form of a slave, being born in human likeness. And being found in human form, he humbled himself and became obedient to the point of death—even death on a cross" (Phil 2:5–8 NRSV). If by being deified we are becoming like the God revealed in Jesus, then here is our model: fully united with God while

1. A good starting place is Wiseman, *John Ruusbroec*, which contains a good translation of most of Ruusbroec's works mentioned in this book.

emptying ourselves for the sake of serving others. This is the answer to the initial question of this section: Now what? Now we return.

The Servants and Friends and Children of God

Is there still more to life and more to us? We thought we finished answering our earlier questions with the attainment of our treasure of total, unmediated, undifferentiated union with God. But if we thought that treasure was ours to keep, our "precious" to obsess over like Gollum in his own little cavernous kingdom, then we still have much to learn about that treasure and the nature of our journey. Oh, it's quite understandable that we would want to remove ourselves to some quiet island—metaphorical and maybe even real—for the sake of meditative contemplation without interruption by the unenlightened world. Even our beloved guide, Reverend John, concludes his masterful *Spiritual Espousals* confessing the longing to "rapidly divest ourselves of the body" and to "flow into the wild waves of the sea" where "no creature could ever bring us back again."[2] But yes, there is still more to life. There is a "now what."

In the *Star Wars* series, Obi-Wan is found having retreated into the deserts of Tatooine. And later, Luke is found having exiled himself to an island on the oceanic planet of Ahch-To. Even dear Reverend John asked permission to retreat from city life and live in a hermitage in the Sonian Forest. The lure of isolation is strong, perhaps especially for those who have been awakened to the bigger reality and a very different way of being. But, as it did through Princess Leia and Rey and Ruusbroec's religious community and others, the world seeks us out and reminds us that it is in desperate need of the treasure we possess and the person we've become on our journey.[3]

We are needed for the Rebellion, for the Resistance, for the kingdom of God coming on earth. In fact, our journey is incomplete—and *we* are incomplete—unless and until we answer this new Call. The new Call is the Call to Return to the world we left behind, a world perhaps we thought and

---

2. John of Ruusbroec, *Spiritual Espousals*, c221–24.

3. For *Star Wars* fans, I do recognize that Obi-Wan's and Luke's exiles were not simply for the sake of enjoying their mystical enlightenment. Still, the point remains that they had retreated, their mystical gifts were needed, and they were summoned by the outside world to return.

even hoped we'd never see again. Our journey is circular, and the circle is broken until we come home.

In his book *The Sparkling Stone*, Reverend John uses the image of servants, friends, and sons of God to describe the stages of our journey. The servants of God represent the Active Life, busy with virtues and disciplines. The friends of God represent the Inner Life, fervently devoted and committed to intimacy with God. And the sons and daughters of God live the Contemplative Life, secure in their divine identity and joyful in the deep rest of the divine embrace. However, these different statuses and "lives" exist in an interesting, non-dualistic relationship with each other: "I call certain people faithful servants, others secret friends, and still others hidden sons. Yet they are all servants and friends and sons for they all serve and love and intend one God and they all live and work out of the free Spirit of God."[4]

What Reverend John is saying here is that, like Russian nesting dolls, one stage exists within the others. On the one hand, the servants contain the destiny of becoming friends and children of God, if only they will make the journey to realize it. And on the other hand, the sons and daughters never leave behind the humility and character that made them servants and then friends. Key for us at this late point in our journey is the second characteristic, that the Active Life and Inner Life are not lost in the Contemplative Life. What makes a Cinderella or an Aladdin heroic is not that they turn their noses up at their former life and embrace the trappings and entitlement of royalty, but that they retain the humble virtues of servanthood and the loving devotion of friendship as they live into their true identity as kingdom heirs.

And so for us, the outward virtues of the Active Life and inward virtues of the Inner Life are required for the enjoyable rest of the Contemplative Life. They must exist in a "nesting" relationship of loving activity, holy yearning, and divine contemplation. This is the treasure—the personhood—we are called to carry back into the world we left behind. As we'll see, the true perfection of our mystical-heroic path is still ahead as we come to live and move *both* inward in the divine Unity *and* outward with the divine Trinity. But first, we have one more threshold to cross, and it is guarded by a challenger who threatens to thwart our whole journey.

4. John of Ruusbroec, *Sparkling Stone*, ll. 384–86.

Refusal and the Return Threshold

As we come to recognize that both our outer and inner virtues—the lessons of the Active and Inner Lives—are intended to exist in mutual relationship with those of the Contemplative Life, we must now set out on the Return journey to a life of perfect love marked by both inward and outward union with God. And yet, the temptation to live only an inward life is now ever-present. Early on, we faced the choice of answering or refusing the Call to this mystical adventure. Then, when we were moving from the Active Life to the long Road of the Inner Life, we faced the First Threshold and its guardian, Reason. That challenge threatened to keep us *in* the known world of activity, and *from* the deepening journey of supernatural adornment and the attainment of our treasure of complete union with our Bridegroom in the divine Unity.

Now, we have another choice: either to answer or refuse the Call to Return. Here we face the Return Threshold, which now stands to keep us *in* the contemplative realm of restful Unity and *from* returning with the Persons of the divine Trinity to the realm of loving activity in the world.

Once again the Threshold seems largely generated by our own decision to cling to Reason, enlightened though it may be. It is a struggle to bring to bear the overwhelming and sublime power of the Inner and Contemplative lives on the corrupt and dying and very superficial world of our initial situation, which at this point seems like a distant memory and perhaps even a nightmare. Our Reason nags us with the questions, "Why return?" and, beyond that, "How to return?"

The real guardian at this Return Threshold, however, is Integration, and he is more a challenger calling us out than a guardian keeping us in. The challenge of Integration is the challenge of living fully and simultaneously the three lives—Active, Inner, and Contemplative—while also reintegrating with the everyday world. Joseph Campbell describes the struggle:

> How teach again . . . what has been taught correctly and incorrectly learned a thousand times, throughout the millennia of mankind's prudent folly? That is the hero's ultimate difficult task. How render back into light-world language the speech-defying pronouncements of the dark? How represent on a two-dimensional surface a three-dimensional form, or in a three-dimensional image a multi-dimensional meaning? How translate into terms of "yes" and "no" revelations that shatter into meaninglessness every attempt to define the pairs of opposites? How communicate to people who

insist on the exclusive evidence of their senses the message of the all-generating void?[5]

Think of all we've been through, all we've learned and seen, all we've *un*-learned and *un*-seen! Our struggle is with the person we have become returning to the world of who we were before we started our journey, the world that had us longing for more to life. Can we now be the ones to exemplify the *via unitiva* we've walked, the ones to sound the Call to Adventure for those who are still now what we once were?

The Return Threshold we must cross consists largely of two temptations: 1) to remain inwardly focused and isolated, i.e., so heavenly minded that we're no earthly good; and 2) to fall back on our natural unity and unadorned abilities, i.e., "having a form of godliness but denying its power" (2 Tim 3:5). Both of these are essentially to dis-integrate, to separate from the divine embrace and go it alone, either by way of detached mysticism or superficial religiosity (and abandonment to various forms of worldliness is always an option as well). Whatever the case, we are facing yet another Call to let go of our need to control, to go on living the simultaneously inward/restful and outward/active life of the divine Tri-Unity, to continue answering our old familiar Call: "See, the bridegroom comes! Go out to meet him!"

By now perhaps we are realizing that this divine Call and mystical earworm is very likely going to be repeated indefinitely, that it is an eternal Call. In fact, this very realization might also constitute our struggle at the Return Threshold: This journey goes on forever?! Yes, the Call is to the continued integration of our ongoing "lives" with the limitless life of God. Across this Threshold is the Return to a life of complexity and challenge, a life now potentially more difficult than the life of our initial situation in the everyday world, which left much to be desired but at least seemed small and manageable. Now there is always more to "See," more ways and places that "the bridegroom comes," more ways and places for us to "go out," ever deeper and higher and grittier and more challenging and life-giving opportunities "to meet him." Or, we can just stay put.

The challenge of Integration and of crossing this Return Threshold, then, is twofold: to return at all; and, if so, to return in our own power or in the power and presence of God. The world to which we must return is the same corrupt world we thought we were leaving behind for good, a world typically hostile to the God to whom we are now betrothed. Nevertheless,

5. Campbell, *Hero with Thousand Faces*, 188–89.

in its very corruption and hostility, the world cries out to God. And so, it cries out to us.

If we will answer the Call to Return and meet the challenges of the Return Threshold, we will find our journey coming to its conclusion in a satisfying but surprising way: one more Life to be lived.

Way-Stop #12: Reflection

We might be taken by surprise here. Some probably started this journey thinking we were heading for where the previous chapter ended, that our destination was the Contemplative Life. We might have been under the impression that that's what mysticism is really about. We do have options. We could withdraw into our own personalized spirituality. Or we could rather easily find a group of like-minded mystics who like to read the same deep books and talk about the same deep things we like, and who share our deep experiences of the mystical. We do love the nonmystical "Muggles," but they just don't get us anymore. And besides that, some of us have experienced a fair amount of pain in the life and world we left behind. Why would we ever dream of going back?

This is where heroism must really step up alongside mysticism. There are plenty of mystics of different times and places and faiths whose mystical turning on and tuning in ultimately led to dropping out. Some had genuine mystical experiences, lived changed lives, and perhaps even became teachers or gurus for others. But they never closed the heroic circle by answering the Call to Return. They welcomed others into their mountaintop experience, but they never carried the holy fire back down the mountain to the people struggling in the darkness and cold. Some such mystics do have good and helpful lessons to offer, but in the end their teaching falls short.

This is why we've chosen Reverend John as our guide for this journey. He leads us into the deepest waters and highest peaks and vastest landscapes that could ever be explored. But then he leads us where only the most heroic mystic could ever go: home. As we'll come to see, the God who holds us in the eternal embrace is walking the streets of our town. This is the highest mystical experience we could ever aspire to. This is the life God is living.

As we begin the Return journey, we might practice regularly praying, perhaps memorizing, and meditating on the words of the Wesleyan Covenant Prayer:

I am no longer my own but yours.
Put me to what you will, rank me with whom you will.
Put me to doing, put me to suffering.
Let me be employed for you or laid aside for you,
exalted for you or brought low for you.
Let me be full, let me be empty. Let me have all things, let me have nothing.
I freely and wholeheartedly yield all things to your pleasure and disposal.
And now, glorious and blessed God, Father, Son, and Holy Spirit,
you are mine and I am yours. So be it.
And the covenant now made on earth, let it be ratified in heaven. Amen.

In addition to simply being a lovely and powerful prayer of surrender and covenant, the words can be a helpful tool for assessing the journey. Am I living only for myself or for God and others? What is God putting me to? With whom am I "ranked" and what is my attitude toward them? Am I aware of God in my "doing"? In my "suffering"? Are there any unexpected or unrecognized ways God wants to employ me? How can I welcome times of being "laid aside for" God, even if the circumstances are not under my control? And so on.

This Covenant Prayer can be an excellent facilitator for honest and probing conversations with God. Such an open, conversational relationship is especially important as we transition into what might be another jarring stage in our mystical-heroic journey. This is where it all starts coming together.

Bearings

- ❖ *Location*: the Return Threshold > Integration > "See, the bridegroom comes! Go out to meet him!" . . . *ad infinitum*

- ❖ *Key Concepts*: the Return; servants of God, friends of God, children of God; the challenge of integration of the Active, Inner, and Contemplative Lives; the challenge of reintegration with the everyday world

- ❖ *Practice*: Wesleyan Covenant Prayer

13

COMMON

The Life God Is Living

During that interminable night... Colonel Aureliano Buendía scratched
for many hours trying to break the hard shell of his solitude.... He
had had to start thirty-two wars and had had to violate all of his pacts
with death and wallow like a hog in the dung heap of glory in order to
discover the privileges of simplicity almost forty years late.

—Gabriel García Márquez, *One Hundred Years of Solitude*

WHAT IS IT WE love about superheroes? Of course we are fascinated
by their powers and riveted by their adventures. Definitely that. But
it isn't their being from another planet or being divine or being brilliant and
super-rich, not their exposure to radiation or their scientific alterations or
their genetic mutations that make superheroes sympathetic figures for us.
It's their humanity.

We connect with superheroes' alienation because we feel alienated.
We identify with their humble or messy origin stories because our origins
are humble and messy. We understand their complicated relationships with
the people and world in which they live and act because we also experience
the complications of people and the world. We are inspired by their struggles with the forces of darkness and evil *around* them, but it is the struggles
within them that we really sympathize with. In short, we aren't fascinated
with superheroes because they are super and other and somehow above us,

as much as because we seem to share something in common. And what we share is commonness.

There is something about the commonness of superheroes that makes us think maybe there's something super in us. This has become more the case as superheroes and their stories become more diverse. There are superheroes from all walks of life, facing struggles that seem very familiar to us, and in a world that also seems familiar. And the more common superheroes become, the more likely we are to find some of their heroism within ourselves. In this way our modern superhero stories serve the purpose that stories of the hero's journey have always served.[1] If that character can find an adventure in this world and the abilities to meet it, maybe we can too. If this character can overcome their alienation or weaknesses or complicated history or inner struggles and do some good in life, perhaps there's hope that we can find meaning and make a difference too.

What we're really seeing is a collision of worlds: the extraordinary in the ordinary, light in darkness, transcendence in immanence. What's more, this collision takes place both within us and around us. Our journey so far has largely addressed the inner struggle. Now, in our Return, we are called to bring what has happened within us back out into the world.

Our full and transformative state of union with God is our treasure—our "superpower," if you will—that is desperately needed in a world that is increasingly fragmented and filled with people who are increasingly disintegrating. We are called to exemplify and nurture the divine union that is unrecognized by so many around us, the way it was once unrecognized by us. It's time to bring the treasure home, to our community and our people, which is where it belongs . . . where we belong. After all, our transformative journey was not for the sake of making us super. It was to make us common.

The Concept of Commonness

The world is calling, and we must answer. We can no longer answer the world's call in the ways we once did, getting what we want and increasing what we have and showing it off to others (see 1 John 2:16). But neither can we claim to love God while turning our backs on our neighbors—our people and our world. Gathering up the treasure of our true, transforming,

---

1. Admittedly, and frustratingly, some film versions of superhero stories are so over the top that any sense of commonness or humanity or the archetypal hero's journey is lost in spectacle and noise.

God-united selves, we must go home. To come home is to answer the Call to a new adventure full of more wonder and beauty and trials and tragedy than anything we might imagine: the adventure of everyday life.

Meeting the challenges of this adventure will require integration within ourselves—simultaneously living the Active, Inner, and Contemplative Lives—which means integration with the life of the divine Unity and the divine Trinity. And this state of fully sharing in the life of God means loving reintegration with the everyday world. This is what now drives our Return journey. In short, this is the life God is living.

Reverend John has a name for all of this integration, for this life that God is living and, so, we should be living. He calls it "the Common Life." It is a fascinating and rather ingenious concept, especially as it overcomes the tension and duality so many mystics encounter between contemplation and action, with most favoring the first at the expense of the second.

The translation of "common" from Ruusbroec's Middle Dutch vernacular (*ghemeyne*) is difficult, as it entails ideas of universality and inclusivity, and it even stretches in Ruusbroec's usage to include eternity. As we'll see, "common" is probably most appropriate since it sweeps in notions of expansive integration and community (as in "common" humanity sharing things "in common"), as well as everyday ordinariness (as in a "commoner" with a "common" house pet). The Common Life is the life God is living, and yet God is living that life in every inch of our ordinary world and every moment of our ordinary history and, as we've discovered, every part of our ordinary selves. So, if the Common Life is to be our life, we must begin to put the pieces together.

The Commonness of the Trinity

The basis for the Common Life is the life and dynamics of the Trinity, the life God is living. According to Reverend John, it goes something like this: The Father ceaselessly births his Son, while the Father is not born (he's the parent). And the Son is ceaselessly being born of the Father, while the Son does not give birth (he's the begotten one). Thus, the Father is always having a Son in eternity, and the Son a Father. And the Father and the Son breathe forth one Spirit, who is the will and love of both of them. The Spirit neither gives birth nor is born but, flowing from both the Father and the Son, is eternally breathed forth (to be clear, there is no time when any of them did not exist). And these three Persons are one God and one Spirit.[2] So, while each divine Person is unique, they are present to each other in common. And characteristics like outflowing love and fruitfulness are common to all three of them, since they work in the power of their shared (common) nature as God.

This is "the commonness of God," which is at work in all of existence *in common*—"in nature and above nature, in all places and at all times, in saints and in mortals, in heaven and on earth, in all creatures whether rational or irrational or material."[3] It is the shared grace and glory and outflowing and presence of the Persons of the Trinity. This commonness of God creates and permeates all of heaven, all of the universe, and all of the natural world. There is no such thing as empty space. As John Wesley beautifully explains,

> The great lesson which our blessed Lord inculcates . . . is that God is in all things, and that we are to see the Creator in the glass of every creature; that we should use and look upon nothing as separate from God, which indeed is a kind of practical atheism; but with a true magnificence of thought, survey heaven and earth, and all that is therein, as contained by God in the hollow of his hand, who by his intimate presence holds them all in being, who pervades and actuates the whole created frame, and is in a true sense the soul of the universe.[4]

That mind-blowing insight bears repeating: God is the soul of the universe. This certainly should not be mistaken for the facile trend of referring to "the universe" as something personal, with the power to grant or withhold our wishes. No, God is the personhood and life in the universe, who nevertheless transcends any number of universes that might exist. From the divine Tri-Unity, to angels, to our own soul and body, to the humble creatures and world around us, God's commonness transcends all and yet is present and particular to each one, for all things exist in and through and for God.[5] Thus, the Holy Trinity is common.

2. John of Ruusbroec, *Spiritual Espousals*, b923–31. This interpretation shows Ruusbroec's Western, Augustinian Trinitarianism in describing the Spirit as proceeding from the Father and the Son (the so-called *filioque*), as opposed to the Eastern view that both the Son and the Spirit proceed only from the Father.

3. John of Ruusbroec, *Spiritual Espousals*, b934, b937–39.

4. Wesley, "Upon Our Lord's Sermon," 1.11.

5. To be clear, Ruusbroec is not advocating pantheism (that all of these created things *are* God). Instead, he is saying that God is fully present to, though independent of, every

The Commonness of Christ

If the Common Life is rooted in the life and dynamics of the Trinity, it is perfectly exemplified and offered in the life of Christ. It is in Christ, still acting as our gracious Helper (and as the world's savior), that we find the Common Life modeled and made available for us. Of course the incarnation of the Son of God—the second Person of the Trinity—is an expression of the aforementioned commonness of God, outflowing in love and fruitfulness. But in Jesus's earthly life and ministry, commonness abounds (again, thinking of "common" as something like the integration of universal, communal, and everyday).

Christ was common in love, in teaching, in guiding, in giving, and in forgiving. His soul and body, life and death, service and sacrifice were and are common. His sacraments and gifts are common. Everything he ever received—whether body and soul, mother and disciples, or cloak and tunic—were always for the common benefit of others. While the torments and suffering and misery he experienced were his alone, the treasures they produced are common, and the glory of his treasure will be common for eternity.

The whole of the commonness of Christ might be summed up in the words "Christ was common in love." Everything that follows is a vivid description of what that looked like for Christ, as well as what it should look like for us. Reverend John offers a striking and insightful portrait of the divine-human Christ living the Common Life:

> With respect to His created soul, Christ was, and is, the greatest contemplative, lover, and enjoyer that ever was; and with respect to His divine nature, He was Himself what one enjoys. Nevertheless, He has never failed anyone, nor ever does, for He is common to all those who desire Him.[6]

Do we think of Christ this way? A great thinker and contemplative? One who loves life and the world and who gets a kick out of people? Someone with a profound gift for enjoying himself and bringing joy to others? One who never fails to be there for us and with us? This is like color and detail being added to the sketch of our beloved Helper. It is fitting that here,

---

part of creation. Whether or not Ruusbroec's view constitutes pan*en*theism is debated, though not especially supported.

6. John of Ruusbroec, *Realm of Lovers*, 2290–93.

at the culmination of our journey, we might really be getting to know him. "I have called you friends," he says (John 15:15).

The Commonness of the Church

Emerging from the commonness of the Trinity and the commonness of Christ is the commonness of Christ's earthly body, the church. Within the blessed community of the faithful we find a mixture of the mystery and power of the church's divine origins and mission with its frail embodiment in fallen humanity among struggling creation. Most of us are all too familiar with this tension. But despite the painful fragility of the vessel, Reverend John refers to the church and its sacraments as the treasure Christ has left on earth—treasure that Christ alone earned by his life and death and which, therefore, should be common to all.[7]

The commonness of the church has, of course, had its ups and downs. Which is all the more reason to look to the periods and movements and saints that embodied total commitment to Christ's mission, to simplicity, peace, unity, divine enlightenment, and faithful charity toward God and all people, and who often sealed their commitment with their blood—their life and their death. The church is (or should be) the communal embodiment of the Active, Inner, and Contemplative Lives, integrated into a corporate Common Life.

Imagine if we considered the church, with its people and sacraments and mission, in terms of (in Ruusbroec's words) Christ's treasure and inheritance, a jewel and secret marvel, and (in Paul's words) "servants of Christ and those entrusted with the mysteries God has revealed."[8] This is the commonness of the church—eternal and universal, yet humble and communal and a gift to the lowliest . . . the most common. In its ideal and at its best, the church shows forth the welcoming embrace and rest of the divine Unity and the active transforming love of the divine Trinity. As the world looks at Jesus and sees God, the world should look at the church and at Christians and see Jesus (and, therefore, God). Though much can and has been said about the church's shortcomings (and Ruusbroec himself does not hold back in his writings), it only brings into stark relief the ideal and the work still to be done.

7. John of Ruusbroec, *Spiritual Espousals*, b1110, b1112.

8. John of Ruusbroec, *Spiritual Espousals*, b1110, b1121, b1127, b1141; see also 1 Cor 4:1.

Way-Stop #13 (Almost There!): Reflection

As we began to talk about returning to the everyday world, we might have thought that meant leaving the mystical stuff behind. Clearly this couldn't have been further from the truth. Instead, with the Return, we are discovering the mysticism of the everyday, of the common. Thomas Merton famously experienced this sort of mystical revelation in the crowded Louisville shopping district at the corner of Fourth and Walnut Streets:

> I was suddenly overwhelmed with the realization that I loved all these people, that they were mine and I theirs, that we could not be alien to one another even though we were total strangers. It was like waking from a dream of separateness. . . . I have the immense joy of being [human], a member of a race in which God Himself became incarnate. As if the sorrows and stupidities of the human condition could overwhelm me, now that I realize what we all are. And if only everybody could realize this! But it cannot be explained. There is no way of telling people that they are all walking around shining like the sun. . . . If only they could all see themselves as they really are. If only we could see each other that way all the time. There would be no more war, no more hatred, no more cruelty, no more greed. . . . But this cannot be seen, only believed and "understood" by a peculiar gift.[9]

This "peculiar gift" is exactly the treasure of union we've discovered on our journey. It allows us to see ourselves and the people and world around us as it all really is. And it can only come from seeing God more and more as God really is.

The practice we would do well to take up in response to this revelation is service. Perhaps the best way we can show others who they really are is to serve them, to treat them like the beloved treasures of God they are. Service is a broad practice that can include: helpful acts done in secret; small or great expressions of generosity; ordinary thoughtfulness and daily kindnesses; hospitality; listening; sharing others' burdens; and any number of creative or mundane ways we acknowledge the sacred worth of others (including animals) and meet some large or small need in their lives. When we serve others we are sharing in the incarnational self-emptying of Christ, who said that he did not come to be served but to serve and give his life for others (Mark 10:42–45).

9. Merton, *Conjectures of Guilty Bystander*, 140–42.

Jesus exemplified what Merton describes, recognizing the light of God in others and loving them in a way that helped them to recognize it in themselves. Christ is the center-point in which the commonness of the Trinity is revealed and upon which the commonness of the church is focused. As with superheroes, yet infinitely more so, it is Christ's commonness that so enraptures and inspires us. It is what saves us: God seeing us as we are and becoming as we are, that he might show us who he is and make us as he is. God getting his hands dirty in our mess, feeling our feelings, bleeding our blood, dying our death. In the incarnation of God the Son we see the ultimate collision of worlds—the extraordinary in the ordinary, light in darkness, transcendence in immanence.

And yet, imagine that collision of worlds happening every place we go. Imagine God incarnated in us. More than enrapturing and inspiring us, and even more than saving us, imagine Christ's commonness making us common. What might it mean for each and all of us to be the location of this grand integration, of the coming together of universality and eternity with community and ordinariness? What might it look like when we bring it all home?

Bearings

- *Location*: the Return > the Common Life > inflowing-resting-outflowing

- *Key Concepts*: commonness as eternal, universal, communal, and everyday; the Common Life; the commonness of the Trinity, of Christ, of the church

- *Practice*: service

14

Coming Home to the True Self

"You are too old, children," said Aslan, "and you must begin to come
close to your own world now."
"It isn't Narnia, you know," sobbed Lucy. "It's you. We shan't meet you
there. And how can we live, never meeting you?"
"But you shall meet me, dear one," said Aslan.
"Are—are you there too, Sir?" said Edmund.
"I am," said Aslan. "But there I have another name. You must learn to
know me by that name. This was the very reason why you were brought
to Narnia, that by knowing me here for a little, you may know me better
there."

—C. S. Lewis, *The Voyage of the Dawn Treader*

T HERE'S NO PLACE LIKE home. It's the lesson Dorothy learns after getting the chance to experience life over the rainbow. She finally returns
to the same Kansas she left behind, but she is not the same Dorothy. Her
journey has led her to the treasure of a deeper and truer understanding of
home, that it is not her isolated farmhouse on the vast plains but the people
who love her. Now she is better able to love them in return. And she is better able to be and love her own true self.

Like Dorothy, Marty McFly goes on an unexpected adventure in *Back
to the Future* that soon leaves him wanting nothing more than to get back
home. Marty's treasure is a similar discovery of the importance and value
of loved ones, and his discovery of that treasure ends up affecting more

than just himself. The interconnectedness of his family and his actions has implications across time, and the courage Marty is able to impart to his father in the past goes on to alter his family's future for the better.

In both of these stories, as in so many others, the treasure of the journey finds its fullest value when it is brought home (whatever "home" might mean). It is only when we bear and employ our treasure among our people and our everyday world that our journey is complete. This is where our true self emerges. Contemporary scholars of heroism, Scott Allison and George Goethels, summarize the way the stages of the hero's journey culminate in this homecoming:

> Hero stories reveal three different targets of heroic transformation: *setting*, *self*, and *society*. These three loci of transformations parallel Campbell's (1949) three major stages of the hero's journey: departure (or separation), initiation, and return. The departure from the hero's familiar world represents a transformation of one's normal, safe environment; the initiation stage is awash with challenge, suffering, mentoring, and transformative growth; and the final stage of return represents the hero's opportunity to use her newfound gifts to transform the world. The sequence of these stages is critical, with each transformation essential for producing the next one. Without a change in setting, the hero cannot change herself, and without a change in herself, the hero cannot change the world.[1]

We might have set out on this journey intent on our own mystic and heroic transformation. But if such a transformation has indeed begun to happen, it will inevitably lead us to transform our little piece of the world. For Indiana Jones, in *Indiana Jones and the Last Crusade*, the Holy Grail is not a treasure because it is a valuable artifact or even because it is the cup of Christ, but because it saves his father's life. And for his father, who has spent his life searching for the grail, its ultimate value is that it brings him and his son together.

As we've come to discover, our journey's true treasure is the person it is helping us to become along the way. Union with God is not something we have; it's who we are. In the words of Symeon the New Theologian (949–1022), "Let us wake up, hesitant ones, so as to be in possession of love, or better, may we become participants in love."[2] It is not enough simply to

---

1. Allison et al., "Metamorphosis of the Hero," 2.
2. Symeon the New Theologian, *Divine Eros*, ll. 410–13.

have love or to *feel* love—we must *participate in* love and *be* love. If we never employ our treasure, which is to say *ourselves*, in loving and serving those around us, we have to wonder if we've really gained any treasure at all. Recalling Christ's Parable of the Wise and Foolish Bridesmaids that has guided us all through our journey, Symeon goes on to urge us, "From henceforth light the lamp, the lamp of your soul, before it grows dark, before the doors of action are closed!"[3] To answer our Bridegroom's Call means ultimately to follow him through the doors of action.

Down from These Heights: The Common Life and the True Self

So we return—treasure attained, a few new scars, elated and exhausted, changed. Coming home is at once a welcome relief and a confusing challenge. We aren't who we were. Some in our sphere will receive our transformation with joy, while others will be suspicious, and some will even walk away. Our old, familiar world will seem different—at once more beautiful and more horrifying, filled with more wonder than we remembered, yet every bit as ordinary and absurd as it ever was. Our circumstances might change—different place, different people, different work or activities—or it might all be the same everyday theater we've acted out for years. Whatever the situation, we must meet it, and meet it fully. This is the Common Life.

The Common Life is the synthesis of outward virtuous activity and disciplines (the Active Life), inner yearning and supernatural adornment (the Inner Life), and transcendent contemplative union (the Contemplative Life), all coming together into a new posture from which we engage the world we departed when we began our journey. From this Common Life comes our true self.

The true self is not something we can point to like the picture that comes together once all the puzzle pieces are in place. Instead, the true self emerges in the working of the puzzle. To employ an old cliché: the true self is a journey, not a destination. But it is a journey toward wholeness, an integration (as opposed to dis-integration) of the self. The true self is the integrating of the Active, Inner, and Contemplative lives; the integrating of our life with God's life; and the integrating of our transforming self with our everyday world. And it's as unique and original as each of us, with our

3. Symeon the New Theologian, *Divine Eros*, ll. 820–23.

own history and abilities and shortcomings and passions and challenges and relationships and daily goings on.

According to Reverend John, the true self looks something like our own unique expression of this:

> The person who is sent by God down from these heights into the world is full of truth and rich in all virtues. And he seeks nothing for himself but only the honor of the one who sent him, and therefore he is just and true in all his actions. And he has a rich, generous foundation which is founded in the wealth of God. Therefore he must always flow into all those who need him, for the living fountain of the Holy Spirit is his wealth and cannot be exhausted. And he is a living, willing instrument of God with which God accomplishes what he wishes in the way he wishes. Such a person does not attribute these accomplishments to himself but gives God the glory. He stands ready and willing to do all that God commands and is strong and courageous in suffering and enduring all that God sends him. *And therefore he has a common life, for contemplation and action come just as readily to him and he is perfect in both.*[4]

We likely need to read that through several times and break it down into its many insightful and instructive pieces. And as we do, it should seem familiar to us: true, just, and virtuous; God-focused and God-filled and overflowing with the life and gifts of the Holy Spirit; an instrument in God's hands and employed for God's glory; strong and courageous; fully united with God in both contemplation and action—common.

The passage is like a scrapbook of our journey, with snapshots of many of our experiences and quests along the way. There we are with Jesus in the school of the kingdom of the soul, learning the virtuous life. There we are being supernaturally adorned, our bodily life and our mental and emotional life and our essential being becoming more Godlike and God-united. There we are in the full embrace of the divine Tri-Unity, being and seeing completely with God. And there we are moving out in loving service among our neighbors and our world and our everyday lives. And the album of all these snapshots together could be titled "My True Self."

This is the genius of John of Ruusbroec's formative path, resisting our tendencies toward dualism at every turn. We find the culmination and perfection of our journey only in the interplay between contemplation and

---

4. John of Ruusbroec, *Sparkling Stone*, ll. 781–92 (emphasis added). See also the translation by Wiseman in *John Ruusbroec*, 184.

action, depth and dynamism. There is a clear expression of Reverend John's simultaneous inflowing-resting-outflowing law of motion. There is also a gentle rebuke of the errors of many of his predecessors and contemporaries in the area of mystical theology, people who consider the mystic journey complete after attaining inward-focused contemplation. We still see that error in many expressions of spirituality and pop mysticism today. Instead, our guide leaves us clear about our heroic obligation to carry the treasure of transformation and union to the needful world, because that's exactly what God is doing.

The picture Reverend John paints is an example of the archetypal hero's journey and its culmination in the Return to the Common Life. As Joseph Campbell explains,

> The hero, therefore, is the man or woman who has been able to battle past his personal and local historical limitations to the generally valid, normally human forms. Such a one's visions, ideas, and inspirations come pristine from the primary springs of human life and thought. Hence they are eloquent, not of the present, disintegrating society and psyche, but of the unquenched source through which society is reborn. The hero has died as modern man; but as eternal man—perfected, unspecific, universal man—he has been reborn. His second solemn task and deed therefore . . . is to return to us, transfigured, and teach the lesson he has learned of life renewed.[5]

In the mystical-heroic journey we have been traveling with Ruusbroec, we see the goal of our own formation as the development of such an "eternal" and "perfected" person drawing from the divine "primary springs of human life" and, ultimately, embodying the good news (gospel) of "life renewed." This is heroism. This is mysticism. And this is the true self.

The subtle image in both Ruusbroec's and Campbell's passages is that of the transfigured Christ, aglow and affirmed with the life of heaven, yet descending the mountain to serve the hurting world (see Mark 9:2–29). The transfiguration reveals a different layer of reality happening at the same time as the reality we see. It isn't just a temporary moment showing how things may one day be. It is the curtain being pulled back on how things always really are—eternal things.

Peter, who wants to set up tabernacles on the mountaintop, isn't wrong in his desire to worshipfully prolong the transcendent event. He's

5. Campbell, *Hero with Thousand Faces*, 14–15.

just wrong in the way he tries to do it. God's way isn't only to meet people in a special tent or temple or on a mountaintop. No, Christ is the tent of meeting. And so, those who are *in Christ* are also tents, each of us the location of the Bridegroom coming to meet others. Aglow and affirmed with the life of heaven, we must also descend the mountain to serve the hurting world.

The Common Life is rooted in Christ as the divine exemplar of Trinitarian spirituality. Again, to be clear, this is the life God is living. And God looks like Jesus. Jesus, who had a family and learned a trade and spent most of his life as a laborer earning a living with calloused hands and a sweaty brow. Jesus, who had an ethnicity and a hometown and a community and friends. Jesus, who, even after being raised from the dead, was mistaken for a gardener. Jesus, the itinerant rabbi and healer and storyteller whose primary message was about the kingdom of God and heaven coming right into the beautiful mess of humanity on earth.

In Jesus, we see a God who was very grounded in the world—enjoying the company of laborers and partyers and the poor and marginalized; far more often found sitting seaside or hillside or walking dusty streets than at the palatial temple; relating the great mysteries of God and God's kingdom through stories about farmers and widows and birds and flowers and weddings and dysfunctional families. Jesus reveals a God who lives a most extraordinary, and yet a very ordinary, life—a common life.

So, if the Common Life is the life God is living, and our journey is about union with God, then the Common Life is the life we are to be living. In Reverend John's later book, *A Mirror of Eternal Blessedness*, he even calls this final stage "the Living Life." It is what Jesus called "eternal life" (e.g., John 6:40) and "abundant life" (10:10), and what Paul called "the life that is truly life" (1 Tim 6:19). They all might have called it "the Getting On with It Life" or, from a marketing standpoint, "the Just Live It Life"!

Our highest state of union, living as God with God, means a life simultaneously flowing into the still embrace of the divine Unity, flowing out in loving activity with the divine Trinity, and resting in deep joy in the midst of it all, whatever comes. This is perfection in love—not in the sense that we have "arrived," since we are forever creatures sojourning and growing into the endlessly expansive landscape and fathomless sea that is God. But this is perfection in the sense of closing the circle of love, of becoming fit for the purpose for which we are made—moving freely and readily in both contemplation and action as we share in the abundant and eternal and peaceful and dynamic life of God.

Arrival: The Peaceable Kingdom, or, There and Back Again

Traditionally, stories like myths and legends and fairy tales often have the hero getting married (usually to royalty) and inheriting a kingdom at the end of his or her journey. That's what Vladimir Propp found in his survey of hundreds of classic wondertales (as he called them), that many ended with the hero returning to marriage and/or the inheritance of a throne. Joseph Campbell's expansive study of myths and legends similarly found the culmination of the hero's journey to be mastery of two worlds or kingdoms, the world of the journey and the everyday world to which the hero returns. And the twist is that the two worlds actually turn out to be different dimensions of one and the same kingdom. For both Propp and Campbell there is a new freedom in the uniting of two beings and two worlds, which Campbell actually calls "freedom to live."[6]

This is precisely what we see in the life and ministry of Jesus Christ. In his incarnation he is the perfect embodiment of the union of God and human, a union he prays his followers will experience as well (John 17). And the main theme of Jesus's ministry was the good news of God's kingdom coming on earth as it is in heaven. Not only are we to be partakers of that kingdom, and also to be means by which it comes, but we are even designated its heirs. "Do not be afraid, little flock," says Jesus, "for your Father has been pleased to give you the kingdom" (Luke 12:32). This is the eternal, awe-inspiring reality that the myths and legends are pointing to.

And it just so happens that this is exactly our experience in the Common Life, lovingly united with our divine Bridegroom and lovingly living in the kingdom of the world that "has become [and is becoming] the kingdom of our Lord and of his Messiah, and he will reign for ever and ever" (Rev 11:15). What this looks like is shalom, a word we might be familiar with as meaning "peace," but which is actually much more. Shalom is indeed peace, but peace as the result of universal flourishing, a deep and expansive peace between us and God and our neighbors and the natural world. It is a life and household and neighborhood and community and nation and world of unity and peace rooted in mutual wellbeing, in caring for each other, in love.

Shalom is the term in the Abrahamic traditions of Judaism, Christianity, and Islam. But the ideal of neighborly love, communal wellbeing, and universal flourishing is also seen (with variations, of course) in the Greek

6. Campbell, *Hero with Thousand Faces*, 205–9.

philosophical concept of *eudaimonia*; in the African teaching of *Ubuntu*; in Buddhist ethical teachings like the *Brahmavihārā*; and in one form or another among small and large cultures and people groups around the world and throughout history. With all that we come up with to divide us, this idea is quite a thing to have in common! Perhaps there's something (or Someone) within all of us urging us toward our common rootedness in divine unity.[7]

However, while this all might sound like romantic idealism, it only comes with hard-fought peacemaking and courageous reconciliation and relentless justice, with difficult conversations and deep listening, at kitchen tables and in town halls and in city streets. It comes from recognizing God and God's work in the world and in our neighbors, and joining God there. It is the Common Life.

Our practice upon our Return might include following the tradition of the pioneering monk, Benedict of Nursia (ca. 480–547), by drawing up a "rule" of life. *The Rule of St. Benedict* helped order monastic communities (and, eventually, much of chaotic Western Europe) according to vows of poverty, chastity, obedience, and stability (remaining in one place), as well as practices like physical labor and fixed hour prayer. The word "rule" should not be thought of as laws, but more like a trellis that guides the growth of plants in a garden. Such a rule would be where the lessons of our journey come together to guide our life back in the everyday world.

Our rule might include vows or values similar to those of Benedict— frugality and generosity, purity of mind and body, accountability to a few others, and dedication to a community. It should draw on our earliest lessons in the school of the kingdom of the soul—humility, justice, charity, compassion, and the rest—and the practices we've acquired along the way—study and *lectio divina*, silence and solitude, celebration and fasting, contemplative prayer, spiritual direction, labor, rest, service, and so on.

With these, as well as the gifts of the Holy Spirit, the great treasure of total divine union, and so much more, we have an embarrassment of riches that can be included in our own Rule of Life. However, it is vital that it consist only of things that are helpful in living our life with God in our everyday world. Better to have a flexible and simple Rule, perhaps with a rotation of a few helpful practices, than to be legalistic about a dense list that is impractical or too complicated to follow. Our Rule should be dynamic,

---

7. We might recall "the spark of the soul" and "prevenient grace" from chapter 1.

addressing our needs in specific moments and seasons of life. Again, the point of it all is a life simply and fully joined with the life of God.

. . . And They Lived Happily Ever After

Living the life God is living. This is where we find our true self. This is the adventure we're made for. Throughout history and across cultures, this is the story humanity has told and retold and longed to be true: that there might be more to life and more to us; that we might find a treasure worth giving our lives for; that we might find an eternal kind of love and live and reign in an eternal kind of kingdom; that we might encounter the gods and perhaps even share in their divinity and activities.

Who knew it could all be true? Oh, we're fine with our myths and legends and wondertales, with our religious rituals and symbols and heavenly hopes. There's nothing wrong—and even much right—with such things. But is it all just a distraction? Is it all fiction, or future, or for someone else? Is it all too fantastical to be real?

Or could it be that this mystical-heroic adventure is what is real? As C. S. Lewis discovered in his conversion from atheism to theism and finally to Christianity, "Here and here only in all time the myth must have become fact; the Word, flesh; God, Man. This is not 'a religion,' nor 'a philosophy.' It is the summing up and actuality of them all."[8] Lewis's realization owed much to conversations with his friend and colleague J. R. R. Tolkien, who coined the term "Eucatastrophe" to describe the sudden, joyous turn in fairy tales from tragedy to a happy ending. Tolkien explained that

> it has long been my feeling (a joyous feeling) that God redeemed the corrupt making-creatures, men, in a way fitting to this aspect, as to others, of their strange nature. The Gospels contain a fairy-story, or a story of a larger kind which embraces all the essence of fairy-stories. They contain many marvels—peculiarly artistic, beautiful, and moving: "mythical" in their perfect, self-contained significance; and among the marvels is the greatest and most complete conceivable Eucatastrophe. But this story has entered History and the primary world. . . . This story is supreme; and it is true . . . Legend and History have met and fused.[9]

8. Lewis, *Surprised by Joy*, 236.

9. Tolkien, *Tree and Leaf*, 71–73. See also Tolkien's poem "Mythopoeia" (mythmaking), which is dedicated to Lewis and which recalls their pivotal late-night conversation and explores and defends the power of myth to reveal eternal truths. Both are found in Tolkien, *Tree and Leaf*.

Maybe the truth, then, is that we've drastically underestimated just how mysterious and epic and fantastic reality actually is. Yes, certainly that is the case.

And it is also the case that each of us is a sub-creator, a mythmaker, the mystic-hero of a tale that is moving toward Eucatastrophe—a turn from tragedy to a joyous ending. Each of us has an untold story within us. It is a story that will remain untold unless we tell it. Our story is hidden with God, and God wants nothing more than for us to come and find it, to tell it, to live it.

Once upon a time . . .

Bearings

- *Location*: the Return > the Common Life > inflowing-resting-outflowing

- *Key Concepts*: dis-integration vs. integration; the true self; the Common Life as perfection in love; *shalom*; myths, legends, and wonder-tales as reality

- *Practice*: Rule of Life

Conclusion

The Voice in the Forest

I went to the woods because I wished to live deliberately, to front only
the essential facts of life, and see if I could not learn what it had to teach,
and not, when I came to die, discover that I had not lived. I did not wish
to live what was not life.

—Henry David Thoreau, *Walden*

T REES CANOPIED THE FAINT trail I followed. Sunlight spilled through
in places, making the green more vivid and highlighting the gold and
brown decaying leaves on the forest floor. I was surrounded by the stuff
of life—reaching trees, warming light, moist air, and a constant chorus of
birdsong. I stopped at a crumbling, moss-covered stone wall that had stood
in those woods for more than 600 years. I continued and came to a meadow
and a calm lake where herons stood watch and a father and son dipped
a fishing line into the water. Then I pressed on—farther, deeper, into the
darker parts of the woods. That's when I heard the voice.

My day had begun in the old university town of Leuven, Belgium. I
was there for a conference and, now that it was over, I stayed on for a few
more days of research and sightseeing. It was Sunday and my plan was a
hike through the Sonian Forest, following in the footsteps of my research
subject, the Blessed John of Ruusbroec.

I sat in a market square enjoying a cup of strong coffee and a pastry
and watching passersby while I waited for my train. The train arrived and
pulled away and I watched gleaming modern buildings and medieval Gothic
churches and graffiti-tagged factories pass by and recede from view. Finally

I arrived in Groenendaal. It didn't strike me as having changed much, at least not in temperament, in the 650 years since Reverend John moved there from bustling Brussels. The train station was boarded up. Weeds grew through cracks in the pavement. A small, white hotel stood proudly behind the station, surrounded by modest houses with satellite dishes on the roofs and children playing in the yards. If there had been a prime for the little Flemish town, it appeared to be long past. It was sleepy and lovely.

I slung my pack onto my shoulder, checked my phone's GPS, and headed for the Ruusbroec Museum. I followed strange roads and walked along a highway, which was fitting as Groenendaal is more a pass-through town than a destination. I eventually found my way to the little museum at the edge of the woods and went in. There appeared to be no one around.

"*Hallo?*" I called. Finally a smiling man appeared from another room and greeted me as he stepped behind the information counter.

"*Sprekt u engels?*" I asked the man.

"*Een betje,*" he confessed, looking a little helpless.

I continued in broken Dutch until another man stepped forward offering stronger English and an eagerness to help. I told him a bit about my research and my love for John of Ruusbroec's teaching. The man confessed to knowing very little about Ruusbroec and nothing about religion. "This is the Ruusbroec Museum, right?" I thought sarcastically. I surmised that the man was more a caretaker than a curator, though he might have been both. Still, he was a cheery host who gave me a map of the forest and a pamphlet about the diverse flora, and then he walked me outside and ushered me on my hike.

Now I stood at the threshold of the deeper journey. And I heard the voice . . . singing. A guitar and a voice, then a few voices. I continued on, assuming a group had brought a guitar along on their own Sunday hike. As I walked, it suddenly struck me that the song was being sung in English. It sounded like home. And more, it was a worship song. The soft music got stronger, the voices multiplying. I continued around a bend and I found a group of twenty-five or thirty people sitting on blankets and camping chairs in a shady clearing—mostly younger adults, some children, and a few middle-aged and older folks. They sang from song sheets and then had a lesson from the Bible, all in English (with various accents). I stood just outside the edge of the group like an unobtrusive tree.

When the young woman who was teaching the lesson finished, she stepped over to me and quietly introduced herself while the service continued. I told her I was a pastor from Texas working on a doctoral dissertation on Ruusbroec, and that I had come to follow him into the woods on this Sunday and was delighted to encounter them and their worship service. She told me they were part of an international church from Brussels, made up of people from all over, and with an American pastor.

She offered me a song sheet and ushered me to a seat. I sang with them, took communion with them, prayed with them and fellowshipped awhile, and met more members and their pastor. Then I was back on my way through the woods. Later I would catch up with several of them at the train station, where we shared what God was doing in and around us at our homes an ocean apart.

In the meantime I enjoyed a long, holy walk through Reverend John's woods. I read passages from works he'd written in that very place. I got off the trail and waded through the thickets and across the spongy carpet of layer upon layer of dead leaves. I prayed for a breath of the same inspiration from the same God who had led the Flemish mystic into the same forest more than 650 years before.

I also recognized the same collision of worlds that Ruusbroec encountered in his day. I was in a foreign country, tired from days of lectures and months and years of pastoring, looking forward to a quiet Sunday hike and some alone time. And yet, there were my people and my community and my churchgoing routine, waiting for me in the woods. Of course I could've ignored the whole scene and passed on by. But God was there, among and within those others, so I had to turn aside and see this strange sight.

We aren't completely sure why Ruusbroec wanted to leave Brussels for a dilapidated hermitage in the Sonian Forest, but it seems clear he wanted simplicity and retreat. Instead, he found community—from the monastery he co-founded to the many seekers he met with and wrote for and welcomed into his own journey on the path to union with God. He went to the woods because he wanted to live deliberately, though he, like any of us, could not anticipate what that might mean. He left man's walls for God's wild, but the world's needs came right along after him. And his voice in the forest transcended place and time to reach multitudes, including our own lives as we've read this book.

Perhaps, like Reverend John and Henry David Thoreau and so many characters both real and imagined, we've gone into some kind of woods to look for something. We wanted something deeper, something more, something less . . . to live deliberately. And yet, whether we were looking for an escape or an adventure, we likely found more than we bargained for. When we leave the walls for the wild, we don't really leave the world behind. And we certainly don't leave ourselves behind.

Beyond our walls is exactly where and when we encounter God most honestly and deeply. And, as we've seen, to encounter God is to encounter our true selves and the world and all the beautiful mess of life. We are caught up in the sublime embrace of heaven, only to find heaven spilling back out onto the earth, and us right along with it. What a journey it all is—a journey that continues and gets richer with the passing of time.

Maybe the lesson of the forest also hits closer to home. Maybe to live what truly is life, the retreat and romance of the forest must eventually be left behind and the old walls must be returned to . . . and dismantled stone by stone. A true mystic is one who is willing to journey with God all the way into the deep mystery of God's loving, transforming embrace. And a true hero is one who is willing to continue with God all the way back into the everyday world of God's loving, transforming service. And to live deliberately only means to step expectantly into the undiscovered landscape of the present moment, what Reverend John called the eternal now.

We likely know some form of the pain and yearning in Maya Angelou's words: "There is no greater agony than bearing an untold story inside you." In the end, we are not after heroism or mysticism or even the true self, at least not for their own sakes. In the end, what we are after is the heroism and mysticism and true self needed to tell our true story. For no one can tell our stories for us, though some will try. I must tell mine. You must tell yours.

Now we've reached the end of this journey; but this is only the beginning of the story.

BIBLIOGRAPHY

Allison, Scott, et al. "The Metamorphosis of the Hero: Principles, Processes, and Purpose." *Frontiers in Psychology* 10 (2019) 1–14.

Athanasius of Alexandria. *On the Incarnation*. Translated by John Behr. Popular Patristics 44B. Yonkers, NY: St. Vladimir's Seminary Press, 2012.

Augustine of Hippo. *Sermons (148–183) on the New Testament*. Edited by John Rotelle. Translated by Edmund Hill. The Works of Saint Augustine: A Translation for the 21st Century 3.5. New Rochelle, NY: New City, 1992.

———. *Teaching Christianity (De Doctrina Christiana)*. Edited by John Rotelle. Translated by Edmund Hill. The Works of Saint Augustine: A Translation for the 21st Century 1.11. Hyde Park, NY: New City, 2014.

———. *The Trinity (De Trinitate)*. Edited by John Rotelle. Translated by Edmund Hill. 2nd ed. The Works of Saint Augustine: A Translation for the 21st Century. Hyde Park, NY: New City, 2012.

Bernard of Clairvaux. "Sermons on *The Song of Songs*." In *Bernard of Clairvaux: Selected Works*, edited by Gillian Evans, Classics of Western Spirituality, 207–78. Mahwah, NJ: Paulist, 1987.

Bonhoeffer, Dietrich. *The Cost of Discipleship*. New York: Touchstone, 1995.

Campbell, Joseph. *The Hero with a Thousand Faces*. 3rd ed. Bollingen Series 17. Novato, CA: New World Library, 2008.

Carlyle, Thomas. *On Heroes, Hero-Worship, and the Heroic in History*. London: Fraser, 1841.

Chesterton, G. K. *Orthodoxy*. Peabody, MA: Hendrickson, 2006.

Coakley, Sarah. *God, Sexuality and the Self: An Essay "On the Trinity."* Cambridge: Cambridge University Press, 2013.

———. "Introduction." In *Re-Thinking Dionysius the Areopagite*, edited by Sarah Coakley and Charles Stang, 1–10. Oxford: Wiley-Blackwell, 2009.

Coakley, Sarah, and Charles Stang, eds. *Re-Thinking Dionysius the Areopagite*. Oxford: Wiley-Blackwell, 2009.

Frye, Northrop. *Anatomy of Criticism: Four Essays*. Princeton, NJ: Princeton University Press, 2000.

Gregory of Nyssa. *The Life of Moses*. Translated by Abraham Malherbe and Everett Ferguson. New York: HarperCollins, 2006.

Herman, David, et al., eds. *The Routledge Encyclopedia of Narrative Theory*. Abingdon, UK: Routledge, 2005.

BIBLIOGRAPHY

Hogan, Patrick. "Archetypal Patterns." In *The Routledge Encyclopedia of Narrative Theory*, edited by David Herman et al., 26. Abingdon, UK: Routledge, 2005.

Irenaeus of Lyons. *Against Heresies*. Edited by Alexander Roberts and James Donaldson. South Bend, IN: Ex Fontibus, 2012.

Isaac of Nineveh. *On Ascetical Life*. Translated by Mary Hansbury. Popular Patristics. Crestwood, NY: St. Vladimir's Seminary Press, 1989.

John of Ruusbroec. *A Mirror of Eternal Blessedness—Jan van Ruusbroec: Opera Omnia VIII*. Edited by Guido de Baere. Translated by André Lefevre. Corpus Christianorum Continuatio Mediaevalis 108. Turnhout, Belg.: Brepols, 2001.

———. *The Realm of Lovers—Jan van Ruusbroec: Opera Omnia IV*. Edited by Joseph Alaerts. Translated by Helen Rolfson. Corpus Christianorum Continuatio Mediaevalis 104. Turnhout, Belg.: Brepols, 1988.

———. *The Sparkling Stone—Jan van Ruusbroec: Opera Omnia X*. Edited by Guido de Baere et al. Translated by André Lefevre. Corpus Christianorum Continuatio Mediaevalis 110. Turnhout, Belg.: Brepols, 1991.

———. *The Spiritual Espousals—Jan van Ruusbroec: Opera Omnia III*. Edited by Josef Alaerts. Translated by Helen Rolfson. Corpus Christianorum Continuatio Mediaevalis 103. Turnhout, Belg.: Brepols, 1988.

John of the Cross. *The Ascent of Mount Carmel*. In *The Collected Works of St. John of the Cross*, edited by Kieran Kavanaugh, translated by Kieran Kavanaugh and Otilio Rodriguez, rev. ed., 101–349. Washington, DC: Institute of Carmelite Studies, 1991.

———. *The Dark Night*. In *The Collected Works of St. John of the Cross*, edited by Kieran Kavanaugh, translated by Kieran Kavanaugh and Otilio Rodriguez, rev. ed., 353–457. Washington, DC: Institute of Carmelite Studies, 1991.

Julian of Norwich. *Showings*. Edited by Edmund Colledge and James Walsh. Classics of Western Spirituality. Mahwah, NJ: Paulist, 1978.

Kierkegaard, Søren. *Purity of Heart Is to Will One Thing*. New York: HarperCollins, 1956.

Lewis, C. S. *The Discarded Image: An Introduction to Medieval and Renaissance Literature*. Cambridge: Cambridge University Press, 2013.

———. *Mere Christianity*. San Francisco: HarperSanFrancisco, 2001.

———. *Surprised by Joy: The Shape of My Early Life*. New York: Harcourt Brace, 1955.

———. *The Weight of Glory and Other Addresses*. Edited by Walter Hooper. New York: Simon & Schuster, 1980.

Lossky, Vladimir. *The Mystical Theology of the Eastern Church*. Crestwood, NY: St. Vladimir's Seminary Press, 1976.

Maximus the Confessor. *Two Hundred Chapters on Theology*. Translated by Luis Joshua Salés. Popular Patristics 53. Yonkers, NY: St. Vladimir's Seminary Press, 2015.

McGinn, Bernard, ed. *The Essential Writings of Christian Mysticism*. New York: Random House, 2006.

———. *The Varieties of Vernacular Mysticism (1350–1550)*. The Presence of God: A History of Western Christian Mysticism 5. New York: Herder & Herder, 2012.

Merton, Thomas. *Conjectures of a Guilty Bystander*. New York: Doubleday, 1966.

———. *New Seeds of Contemplation*. New York: New Directions, 2007.

Mulholland, M. Robert. *Shaped by the Word: The Power of Scripture in Spiritual Formation*. Nashville: Upper Room, 2001.

Origen of Alexandria. *Origen: Contra Celsum*. Translated by Henry Chadwick. Cambridge: Cambridge University Press, 1980.

Payton, James. *Light from the Christian East: An Introduction to the Orthodox Tradition.* Downers Grove, IL: InterVarsity, 2007.

Pelfrey, Robert. *Spiritual Formation as the Hero's Journey in John of Ruusbroec.* Abingdon, UK: Routledge, 2022.

———. *Still Moving: The Journey of Love's Perfection.* Eugene, OR: Resource, 2017.

Propp, Vladimir. *Morphology of the Folktale.* Translated by Laurence Scott. Austin: University of Texas Press, 1968.

Pseudo-Dionysius. *The Celestial Hierarchy.* In *Pseudo-Dionysius: The Complete Works*, edited by Colm Luibheid, translated by Colm Luibheid and Paul Rorem, Classics of Western Spirituality, 143–91. Mahwah, NJ: Paulist, 1987.

———. *The Mystical Theology.* In *Pseudo-Dionysius: The Complete Works*, edited by Colm Luibheid, translated by Colm Luibheid and Paul Rorem, Classics of Western Spirituality, 133–41. Mahwah, NJ: Paulist, 1987.

Rilke, Rainer Maria. *Letters to a Young Poet.* Translated by Joan M. Burnham. 2nd ed. Novato, CA: New World Library, 2000.

Stang, Charles. "Dionysius, Paul and the Significance of the Pseudonym." In *Re-Thinking Dionysius the Areopagite*, edited by Sarah Coakley and Charles Stang, 11–22. Oxford: Wiley-Blackwell, 2009.

Symeon the New Theologian. *Divine Eros: Hymns of Saint Symeon the New Theologian.* Translated by Daniel Griggs. Popular Patristics 40. Crestwood, NY: St Vladimir's Seminary Press, 2010.

Thomas à Kempis. *The Imitation of Christ.* Translated by William C. Creasy. Notre Dame, IN: Ave Maria, 2017.

Tolkien, J. R. R. *Tree and Leaf.* London: HarperCollins, 2001.

Watson, Kevin. *Perfect Love: Recovering Entire Sanctification—The Lost Power of the Methodist Movement.* Franklin, TN: Seedbed, 2021.

Wesley, John. *Explanatory Notes upon the New Testament.* Salem, OH: Schmul, 1975.

———. *A Plain Account of Christian Perfection.* Kansas City, MO: Beacon Hill, 1966.

———. "The Principles of a Methodist Farther Explained." In *The Works of John Wesley: The Methodist Societies: History, Nature and Design*, edited by Rupert Davies, The Works of John Wesley Bicentennial Edition, 9:227. Nashville: Abingdon, 1989.

———. "The Scripture Way of Salvation." In *Wesley's 52 Standard Sermons*, edited by Nathanael Burwash, 438–47. Salem, OH: Schmul, 1988.

———. "Upon Our Lord's Sermon on the Mount—Discourse III." In *Wesley's 52 Standard Sermons*, edited by Nathanael Burwash, 228–39. Salem, OH: Schmul, 1988.

Willard, Dallas. *The Divine Conspiracy: Rediscovering Our Hidden Life in God.* New York: HarperCollins, 1998.

———. *The Great Omission: Reclaiming Jesus's Essential Teachings on Discipleship.* New York: HarperCollins, 2006.

———. *Renovation of the Heart: Putting on the Character of Christ.* Colorado Springs: NavPress, 2002.

Wiseman, James, ed. *John Ruusbroec: The Spiritual Espousals and Other Works.* Classics of Western Spirituality. Mahwah, NJ: Paulist, 1985.